The Woman's Day Book of Hints for Cat Owners

The Woman's Day Book of Hints for Cat Owners

by Jean Burden

Illustrations by Carol Selkin

Fawcett Columbine ★ *New York*

For Linus and Lucy

THE WOMAN'S DAY BOOK OF HINTS FOR CAT OWNERS

Published by Fawcett Columbine Books, a unit of CBS Publications,
the Consumer Publishing Division of CBS Inc.

ISBN: 0–449–90033–9

Printed in the United States of America

First Fawcett Columbine Printing: October 1980

10 9 8 7 6 5 4 3 2 1

Preface

All the material in this book comes from three sources: my articles in *Woman's Day*, whose pet column I have had the privilege of writing since 1973; my voluminous files and library on cats; and my head.

Since the age of six, when my first cat found me sitting on the front porch, I have lived with cats, observed them, studied them, experienced life with them. My alter ego, my totem, is CAT.

This book does not pretend to be an encyclopedia of feline lore, but it does try to zero in on the kinds of information cat owners need in order to be good to their pets, to understand them from *their* point of view, and to enjoy them more fully.

Cats remind us that there is still an element in life that is untamable and free. Through them, we are able to get in touch with that same element in ourselves. It is no small gift they give us. This book—and the others I have written about them—is my small "thank you" for the privilege of sharing my life with these beautiful, mysterious creatures.

J. B.

Acknowledgments

Thanks are due to Pet Pride for clarification on several obscure points; to Morris Animal Foundation for their latest research on feline diseases; to John David Chudacoff, D.V.M., for reading and editing the section on "Health, Good Living and Illness"; to New American Library for allowing me to use excerpts from a chapter of my book, *The Classic Cats* (1975), which first appeared in *Woman's Day*, and for permitting me to refer to *The Classic Cats* in the section on breeds; and, finally, to Louise Egan Steele and Norene Harris for helping me with the enormous job of excerpting these pieces of information from the hundreds of articles on cats I have written for *Woman's Day* over the past many years.

Contents

VI   OWNER RELATIONSHIP AND RESPONSIBILITY

CHAPTER ONE

Background and Breeds

A Bit of History

It is thought that the cat first pawed its way toward domestication as early as 3000 B.C. in Egypt. The ancient tabby could have been a descendant of the Kaffir (or Caffre) cat, a small yellow wildcat with faint black marks and bands and a tail ringed with black.

Soldiers, sailors, and traders were probably responsible for scattering the Egyptian cat throughout the Mediterranean. The cat is found in Greek and Roman mythology, though it occupies a far less lofty perch than in Egypt, and by the fifth century A.D., the cat turned up in Europe and the British Isles.

The cat moved in the other direction—into Asia—as early as the fifth century B.C., probably smuggled out of Egypt because of its rat-hunting proclivities, and ended up in China around the second century B.C. From China it moved over to Japan.

*

The answer to why a cat is usually called "she" lies in the history and mythology surrounding this fascinating animal. Down through time, the cat has been much more associated with feminine forms such as the Egyptian goddess Pasht (or Bastet), who had a cat's head, and the Norse goddess Freya, who rode a chariot drawn by two black cats. Freya became the central figure in a Teutonic cult given to bacchanals and colorful sin, which was severely frowned on by Christianity but which spread through Western Europe. Because a cat's eyes dilate at night, it has also been identified with Diana, goddess of the moon.

Cats have been associated throughout history with the polarities of divinity and evil. In ancient Egypt the cat became the chief of sacred animals, along with the baboon and crocodile. The cat was loved, protected, even worshipped. Anyone who was so foolish as to kill a cat was himself executed. When tombs were excavated, thousands of mummified cats were uncovered.

In the fourteenth century, encouraged by the Church, the cat became associated in Europe with Satan, witches, and demons. If you merely owned a cat, you were suspect. Countless numbers of cats were put to death—to say nothing of witches. The chief agent to turn the tide of public opinion, and to convince even the Church, was the invasion of the black rat, bringing with it the plague. Rats also destroyed crops and even attacked children. Who could stop them? Enter the cats! Slowly the church relaxed its persecution, and the cat assumed its rightful place as man's loyal companion and most ardent vermin-killer.

But of all domestic animals, the cat has changed the least from its wild ancestors. For over five thousand years (we think) *Felis catus* has lived with man. But even today it has changed very little from its jungle forebears. Loving as a cat can be, it has in its genes something akin to the tiger. The wise cat owner knows this well.

The Cat as Hunter

Authorities do not wholly agree how far back the household cat goes, but there are fossil records that show that it was fully evolved at least ten million years ago, and that it has changed very little, if at all, in body structure since then.

The cat's long history may be partly explained by the fact that it has always been a highly developed mammalian predator. Tom and Tabby today are just as efficient hunters as their ancestors, even if the need for such activity has been set aside in favor of listening for the can opener.

If your cat brings you a "present" of a dead mouse or bird, do not punish it. It is not aware of your sensibilities. It lives by its own. Smother your distaste, dispose of the carcass as speedily as possible, and don't forget to lavish praise on Puss.

If you *want* your cat to hunt (as do some farmers who keep cats to kill vermin), don't withhold food in the mistaken idea that starvation will sharpen its skills. Some cats are excellent hunters and pursue the sport all the time (sometimes, in my opinion, out of boredom), while others never make the team.

It is possible to pamper the hunting instincts of a household cat even if it never goes out. Provide it with toys that stimulate stalking and pouncing, such as a catnip mouse, a Ping-Pong ball, or just a wadded-up piece of stiff paper. (It must have the proper crinkly sound—newspaper is too soft.)

Breeds*

Through natural evolution and with a probable assist from man, "breeds," or families of cats with distinct characterizations setting them apart from other families, began to develop.

When the feline newcomers to England interbred with the small British wildcat, even more changes undoubtedly took place. Although there is written proof that cats were shown for "beauty and breed" at an English fair as early as 1598, officially pedigreed ones have a history of only about one hundred years. In 1871 the first official cat show in London was held at the Crystal Palace. In 1887 the British formed the first cat club, which grew into the Governing Council of the Cat Fancy, the group that developed standards for the various breeds. As the fancy became established in America, various associations were founded.

---

* For further details, see *The Classic Cats,* by Jean Burden (New American Library, 1975).

Since dogs entered the home of man thousands of years before cats, centuries of crossbreeding have given them many more shapes and sizes than the relative newcomer to the hearth. Nowhere in the cat family can you see such a variance as exists, for instance, between a miniature Poodle and a St. Bernard.

*

A cat is always easily recognized as a cat. Every representative of *Felis catus* fits within a basic pattern. What principally distinguishes one breed of cat from another is coat and color.

*

The number of mixed-breed cats far exceeds the purebreds. Of the approximately forty million cats in the United States, only about forty thousand are registered as pedigreed.

*

If you're thinking of adding a purebred to your life (See "If You Want a Really Classy Cat") and you're about to look over the feline Four Hundred at your first cat show, you'd better do a little homework ahead of time.

*

Go to your local library and look up the official standards for the classic breeds usually seen in show competition. In poring over the standards you'll be intrigued with the variation of colors in the coats—shaded cameo, red chinchilla, black smoke, tortoiseshell, blue cream—it's like a catalogue of exotic rugs from an ancient bazaar.

*

The purebreds' eyes, too, are judged for their vivid golds, yellows, coppers, greens, and blues. Even some of their paw pads must be a specific lavender pink. A color-blind judge need not apply at any cat show.

*

If the cat's coat is not a solid color (or perhaps a combination of two or three solid colors), the pattern will often be tabby.

*

The word "tabby" can be traced back to "Atabi," a silk ribbed with wavy lines produced in ancient Baghdad. Tabby markings, found on both household and purebred cats, come in a variety of colors.

*

In cat show judgings of the purebreds, there are two accepted tabby patterns, the classic and the mackerel.

*

14

There's a butterfly on the shoulders of the classic tabby, formed by the broad dense markings that also evenly band its legs, give it necklaces on the neck and upper chest, and three distinct stripes down its spine. It also sports a double row of "buttons" on its chest and an intricate letter *M* on its forehead.

The mackerel tabby features a saddle on its back formed by dense but narrow pencilled markings. Distinct necklaces, like chains, are also featured, as well as narrow bracelets that come up from its evenly barred legs to the body markings. It too has an intricate letter *M* on its forehead—for "miaow," maybe?

As every careful cat owner with comb and brush knows, the feline population is made up of shorthairs and longhairs, with a few going to only medium length.

The length of a cat's hair may loom large in your search for a purebred to call your own, either because of personal aesthetic preference or grooming requirements. The longhair will take a bit more attention that the shorthair.

Here's the short and the long of it in the breeds currently accepted for show competition in the United States.

Basic Shorthairs

The Abyssinian: The Aby, as it is called, comes in two colors, ruddy and red, ticked in shades of darker brown and black for the ruddy and in chocolate brown for the red. Its body is long and lithe. Big ears and large almond eyes in gold or green complete the picture of this svelte beauty.

Closely resembling its probable ancient ancestors depicted in early Egyptian paintings and statues, the Aby is often seen sitting as if it were posing for an artist, neck arched, feet together.

Despite its resemblance to a miniature cougar (or "Little Lion," as it's sometimes referred to), this highly intelligent cat is unusually affectionate and loving. Mischievous but not destructive, it likes people and gets along well with other pets.

American Shorthair: When you first see this classic cat perhaps you'll say to yourself: "My Felix looks a little like that, and so does the stray my sister just took in."

Many "cat cats" (or mixed breeds) in the United States do resemble it, but the American Shorthair, whose ancestors came over on the Mayflower to protect the Pilgrims' grain from rats, has been carefully and selectively preserved as a distinct breed. Considered by some to be the first fully domesticated cat, the American Shorthair's ancestry, it is thought, goes back to the early felines of Rome.

*

With a round head and slightly squared muzzle, full chest and short, sturdy legs, this cat is the picture of working strength. Gorgeous coat colorings and markings are the purebred's most exciting feature.

*

Even-tempered and intelligent, robust and loving, the American Shorthair is tolerant with children, and a fine pet to have around the house.

Bombay: This relatively new variety, a cross between a Burmese and an American Shorthair, has a coat that looks like shiny black patent leather, and eyes of great depth and brilliance, ranging in color from yellow to deep copper. Of average size, with a round head and wide-apart eyes, the Bombay has a pleasing personality.

Burmese: The golden-eyed "Burm," with its satiny, sable-brown coat, brings to mind a little brown bear.

Descended from a shorthaired brown cat brought here from Burma in 1930, the Burmese breed was scientifically developed by first crossing it with a Seal Point Siamese.

Medium sized, with expressive eyes and a sweet face, the healthy Burmese has a glossy sheen to its coat.

*

Open and friendly, the Burmese requires human company to nourish its happiness. Make it your *only* pet, though. It's jealous of other cats.

Colorpoint Shorthair:　These delicately colored hybrids, in pastel shades, are a triumph of breeding. Applying genetic principles, breeders have succeeded in combining new point colors with the Siamese-type body and conformation.

*

With vivid blue eyes, they have coats of cream or white with points (darker markings) of deep red, black, brown, blue, or silver.

*

Though not as rambunctious as the pure Siamese, the Colorpoint Shorthair has a similar personality.

Egyptian Mau:　This graceful little cat, long, lithe, and Oriental like the Abyssinian, was developed in the United States from cats brought from Cairo. Evenly spotted with banded legs, its pale coat has a lustrous sheen. Only two colors are accepted: silver with black spots on a silver ground, and bronze with bronze spots on a tawny ground. This agile, intelligent cat almost named itself. "Mau" is how "Miaow" is said in its quiet voice.

Exotic Shorthair:　If you like the beauty and colors of a Persian without the fuss of its excessively long hair, this is the hybrid for you—a cross between the Persian, with its body conformation, and the American Shorthair. It has the best of both personalities.

Havana Brown:　This tobacco-colored cat that reminded somebody of a fine Havana cigar originated in England, not Cuba. A result of conscientious breeding, the Havana is part Seal Point Siamese, Black British Shorthair, and Russian Blue.

*

Rich brown right down to its whiskers, its eyes are a deep green. With an elfin expression on its slightly Oriental face, this cat is charming, but its prankish behavior may have it leaping over your furniture or pawing at your art objects.

Japanese Bobtail:　This slant-eyed beauty, with its stumpy pom-pom tail, landed on the American scene in 1969.

Slim and long-legged, the ideal Bobtail is traditionally *Mi-ke* (pronounced mee-kay), meaning tricolor, in black, white, and red-orange.

*

Considered good luck in its native Japan, this talky, attention-getting cat makes a good companion and is a conversation piece in any home.

Korat: The first thing you'll notice in this good-luck cat from Thailand will be its oversized iridescent green-gold eyes and its heart-shaped face.

*

Slim, with silver-tipped blue-gray fur, the purebred Korat must be able to trace its ancestry to Thailand, which makes it known as the "cat with a passport."

*

Of a quiet nature, the Korat makes a gentle, responsive pet who likes to snuggle next to its owner and prefers to be the only cat around.

Oriental Shorthair: This hybrid produced by the cross-breeding of Siamese, American Shorthairs, Colorpoint Shorthairs, and still other Oriental Shorthairs, has the elegance and conformation of the Siamese with more exotic colors and patterns—from lavender smoke and chocolate to blues and reds.

Rex: A mutation perpetuated by man through a carefully planned genetic breeding program, the Rex is referred to as "steel covered with velvet."

*

Appearing in many colors and patterns, its fur looks freshly marcelled because it has no guard hairs. Its coat resembles that of a Rex rabbit; hence its name.

*

An unusual feature of its whippetlike body is its long and sparsely furred tail.

*

A loving and lovable pet, the Rex insists upon having its owner's attention and is one of the most demonstrative of all cats.

Manx: There's something missing in this classic cat, which hails from the Isle of Man, off the coast of Great Britain. It doesn't have a tail. That is the famous "rumpy" variety. A "stumpy" Manx has a stump of one to five inches long. A "longy" Manx has a full-length tail. Only the rumpy can be accepted for shows.

The rumpy Manx's rather high, rounded posterior and long hind legs has earned it the nickname of "bunny cat." Though some claim it even hops like a bunny, its actual distinctive gait is more like that of a waddling duck. Its short, thick fur comes in many colors and patterns.

*

Highly intelligent, with a sweet and expressive voice, it is wonderful with children. And if you live on a farm, consider the Manx as a working pet. It's reputed to be the best "ratter" of all domesticated cats.

Russian Blue: Queen Victoria owned a pair of Russian Blues, the plush-coated emerald-eyed beauties said to be descendants of cats in the royal house of Russia.

*

Its unique double coat of blue-gray tipped with silver begs to be touched. As you stroke the fur you can make designs in it, as you can in beaver fur.

*

Easy to care for, quiet and amiable, the Blue is especially suited to apartment living. Though it can sometimes be a clown, it is basically a poised and dignified pet.

Siamese: The most striking thing about the Siamese, often called "The Prince of Cats," is its remarkable coloring: a pale fawn or cream coat set off by points (dark areas) on the face, ears, feet, and tail.

*

Its body is sleek and graceful, topped with a fine, wedge-shaped head.

*

First shown in America in the early 1900s (it came here from Hong Kong via England), it has been one of the most popular breeds ever since.

*

Described as the cat with the small-boy personality, the mischievous Siamese entertains its loving owners with its hijinks, its noisy conversations, its agility, and its independent, one-track mind.

*

The Siamese has the reputation as being one of the most interesting, intelligent, and affectionate cats that reside with man.

The Longhairs

Balinese: First called the Longhaired Siamese, the Balinese (which never saw Bali) was developed as a breed here in the United States from a mating of mutations, both offsprings of purebred Siamese.

This long-haired enchantress, with its plumey tail and a ruff framing its Siamese face, is easy to keep looking at its best, for its long coat lies naturally and requires no complicated grooming.

It has the same appealing personality as its Siamese cousins.

Birman: As befits its title of "Sacred Cat of Burma," this beauty comes equipped with a complete set of immaculate white gloves. At first glance, its points and long fur appear the same as the Himalayan's, although it is not so stocky and the body color has a golden tinge to it.

Easygoing yet full of activity, the graceful, magnificent Birman has a small voice but a tigerlike gait. It makes a fine, endearing pet.

Himalayan: Often called the "ultimate cat," this monument to genetic perseverance looks like a Persian in a Siamese overcoat.

Simultaneously developed in America and England, this hybrid has the cobby (the fancier's term for low and heavyset body) of the Persian and light body coloring and points of the Siamese.

It combines the best of both its families in personality too—it's neither as rambunctious as the Siamese nor as reticent as the Persian.

A quiet conversationalist, the Himalayan is affectionate though aloof— lovely to look at, delightful to own. And its long fur doesn't mat.

Maine Coon Cat: A big, shaggy, highly intelligent cat, the pride of Down East is a natural breed whose lineage goes back on one side to British Short-hairs that came over on the Mayflower, and on the other to longhairs probably brought by sailors from Turkey over a century ago.

Muscular and sturdy, this semi-longhair has a rough-napped coat and a long, bushy tail. It comes in various colors and tabby markings. Agile, alert, charming, it's well suited for cold winters and rugged landscapes.

Persian: Underneath the extravagantly glorious coat of this gentle aristocrat of the feline world is the low, heavyset, thick-legged body of a peasant. This sweet-faced, brilliant-eyed combination of sturdy squareness and opulent outwardly-flowing fur is an aesthete's delight. It comes in thirty-five color and pattern possibilities.

As if aware of its own elegance, the Persian will amiably stand still for its daily grooming, often a tedious and time-consuming task for its proud owner.

Sweet and dignified, it is usually reticent toward everybody but its owner. A good indoor cat, perfect for apartment living, it is not too crazy about children.

Turkish Angora: Believed to be one of the oldest of the natural breeds of domestic cats, the modern-day Angoras are direct descendants of several pairs brought to the United States in the 1960s from the zoo at Ankara (formerly Angora), Turkey, which had been conducting a fine breeding program for its ancient feline treasure.

Though Angoras come in other colors too, only pure white is recognized in the American show ring.

The Angora is often confused in the public's mind with the Persian, but there's a clear distinction between the two. The Angora's head is more triangular than the Persian's, its nose is longer, and its round eyes may be slightly slanted. Besides, its fur is finer and silkier than that of a Persian, though just as difficult to groom.

Responsive and loving, polite, and a little deferential, the Angora can be trained, sometimes even to retrieve. Like some other pure-white cats, though not all, it may be deaf.

Though they won't be competing officially, other recognized breeds, such as the British Shorthair, the Supilak, the Chartreux, and others, may also appear at major cat shows for your inspection and admiration.

And you haven't seen everything yet. With our knowledge of genetics, and the new mutations that inevitably occur, there is a profusion of possibilities for new breeds.

The standards for existing breeds are subject to change, too. If you compare today's champion Siamese or Persians with photos of the best of those breeds just ten or twenty years ago, you'll see that the interpretation of the ideal inevitably alters with the passing years. For example, the ideal Siamese head has become flatter and more wedge-shaped over the years.

If You Want a Really Classy Cat

Most people have never thought of paying money for a cat. To them, a cat is a gray tabby that followed them home or a black imp they couldn't resist at the SPCA.

There are no better pets in the world than "cat cats," but there *is* a feline elite, and more and more people are learning about it with the idea of becoming the proud possessor of one of its members.

The primary question you must answer before you make the first move toward acquiring a pedigreed cat is not what kind of cat you want, but what kind of cat person you are.

There are three types: (1) the person who loves cats and just wants a nice, handsome pet, with no thought of either showing or breeding it; (2) the person who would like to breed cats; (3) the cat fancier who not only wants to breed cats but would like to show them for the joy of competition and, it is hoped, improvement of the breed.

If you have never owned a purebred cat before, it isn't a bad idea to break into the field by first buying a pet-quality kitten.

Is a pet-quality kitten a substandard animal? Not really. It merely means that the kitten has a slight fault *by show standards*.

None of these faults—too closely set eyes in a Persian, for instance, or a Siamese's kinked tail—would hinder the joy of ownership.

The first purebred cat I ever owned was a red Persian named Jason whose only flaw was a nose a fraction of an inch too long.

*

A good pet-quality kitten generally costs between thirty-five and seventy-five dollars. Rare breeds may be higher.

*

A cat sold for breeding purposes may also carry some flaws, but it has proved it will produce championship progeny because of the excellent bloodlines in its pedigree.

*

The complexities of these genetics are not going to be absorbed by you in a minute, so you will do well to do some reading and investigating before you settle on the type of cat.

*

The best buy is a female. You can select a stud cat later, and pay a stud fee. A female is easier than a male to care for, unless you are prepared to handle the male's spraying habits.

*

Much later, when you are no longer a novice, you can learn how to cope with a pair.

*

The price of a female? Depends entirely on rarity of breed and excellence of type—from around $250 to $2500. Cheap they're not.

*

Don't expect to make a fortune breeding cats. The upkeep and maintenance of a cattery are costly.

*

If you develop a world-famous cattery for one particular breed, you may be able to demand a high price for your cats.

*

If you are just plain folk down the street who happen to have a cat with papers, you will be lucky to break even.

*

Money is not the object in cat breeding; the joy of developing fine specimens of a breed is the name of the game. Most expensive and elite of all purebreds is the cat who has the color, body conformation, health, and élan to win honors at cat shows. It can also be bred, of course.

If your heart is set on a future grand champion, you may have to do some shopping. Kittens that grow up to satisfy the standards of their breed aren't born every minute.

Which breed is for you and where can you find it? To go about this project in the approved and ultimately profitable manner will take you more than a spare weekend.

The worst thing you can do is call on your neighbor whose cute but unregistered Siamese with the crossed eyes has just had another litter, and fall for the first kitten that toddles toward you.

Stay clear of classified ads in your daily newspaper or pet stores. The antecedents of such so-called purebreds are too hard to trace.

The right way to go about this venture is to attend a cat show—preferably many cat shows.

You may start out with the idea that you want a Persian. Fine, but at the show you will not only see an incredible spectrum of colors in the Persian breed; you will also be exposed to other breeds you may never have heard of.

Stop and chat with the breeders. Take away some of their literature. You will want to know the advantages and disadvantages of the breeds. For example, longhairs require much more grooming than the shorthairs. They shed more.

See your favorite in the context of all the other cats. You may come away preferring a Silver Tabby Shorthair or a Burmese.

Go to another show and keep on looking. In the meantime, get some books and read up on the breeds that attract you most.

*

Write to a few breeders who advertise in the cat magazines. Remember, as you narrow your choices, that you must choose not only for looks but for

temperament. A Siamese does not act like a Manx or a Persian like an Abyssinian.

The next step is to settle on a breeder. If you have made a friend at one of the cat shows, go back and ask to visit his or her cattery.

A breeder whose cattery has been given a seal of approval by the Pet Pride organization, the national educational and welfare organization devoted solely to cats, has a definite plus.

For obvious reasons it is important to visit the cattery rather than transact business at a distance. The cattery should be clean, light, and well ventilated. Cages should be large and comfortable. They should not stink of cat, though with stud cats there may be some odor. In other words, the cattery should be an attractive home for the cats, not a "kitten mill."

The cats themselves will reflect good care and love. They should be healthy. Be suspicious of runny eyes or noses, dull coats, or dirty ears. A sneezing cat is a menace; it probably has a respiratory disease that will infect the whole colony. Also, look out for cats that scratch themselves; this might mean fleas or something worse.

If you find it hard to make a choice, ask the breeder to help you.

Assuming all are healthy, how will you be able to guess which one has the disposition you want? Try picking one that is not afraid, that comes toward you to make friends quickly, that purrs when you touch it. (See "How to Choose a Kitten.")

If you are shopping for a show cat, you should make inquiries as to just what constitutes show quality in your choice. You don't want to pay a fancy price for an unfancy cat.

*

Three months is the preferred age to adopt a purebred cat.

*

When you make your final selection, be sure you have a written inoculation record.

*

Your breeder should be willing to give you a guarantee that the kitten has no congenital defects.

*

The first thing you do on your way home with your new glamour puss is stop off at the veterinarian for a complete checkup.

*

If an immediate examination turns up anything wrong, some breeders may reimburse the veterinarian's fees.

*

The vet can also tell you about grooming and diet if your breeder has not.

*

If, after you have had your kitten a few weeks, you decide it is not for you, for whatever reason, take it back to the breeder. You are not doing it any favor by keeping it. Compatibility works both ways.

*

Now begin *your* responsibilities as the owner of a purebred cat. If your cat is of pet quality, you will be asked to alter it at the proper age before you can receive the cat's papers from its breeder.

*

If your cat is for breeding purposes, you must breed it carefully.

*

If Tabby is of show quality, you should follow through and show her. But, if she doesn't win all the prizes, you will be expected to love her just the same. You, of course, must give her good nutrition, comfortable housing, regular veterinary checkups, and lots of attention.

*

Even if it doesn't grow up to be a grand champion, a cat's a cat for all that. And a purebred cat is the classiest cat of all.

Is Your Cat the Show-Biz Type?

At one time the only people to enter cat shows were the owners of purebred varieties such as the Persian, Siamese, Manx, or Abyssinian. Not so these days.

*

Except for cats that have been declawed and cats that are pregnant, just about any feline that can swish a tail is eligible for a cat show. Cat shows are no longer the exclusive province of high society.

*

The Cat Fanciers' Association, one of several groups that register purebred cats, sponsors more than two hundred shows a year and receives entries for more than sixty thousand cats.

*

Some shows are select—for purebreds only or household cats only. Generally, though, the shows are large, all-encompassing affairs with subdivisions for purebreds, altered purebreds, and household pets (mixed breeds).

*

If your cat is registered and purebred, she is entered in the Championship Class, provided she is eight months old or older; if she is between four and eight months, she is registered in the Kitten Class.

*

If your cat is *not* registered but is still a purebred, she is limited to the Household Pet Class.

*

If you're interested in entering a cat show, make a call or write a note to your local cat-fancier group or humane society and find out when the next event will be taking place and where.

*

Many of the shows occur in the fall and winter, when the animals' coats are at their luxuriant best.

*

When you apply you will be asked to pay an entrance fee, usually about twelve dollars, and you will be instructed where and when to bring your cat.

*

Be prepared for an early start. Most entries have to be at the gate by 7 A.M.

Get Your Contestant Ready

Take a day off and prepare your cat for the big day.

*

Tabby must be squeaky clean, in good health (there will be an examination by a very fussy veterinarian on the morning of the show), and combed and brushed so that every hair glistens.

*

A few days before the show give your cat a bath and see that her nails are clipped and her teeth and ears are in good shape.

*

No ear mites allowed, and no fleas!

*

If you have any doubts about Tabby's show-girl appearance, take her to a groomer. It may be a little expensive, but it's worth it.

*

Like any model, Tabby will need certain personal necessities to see her through the day. Pack her food and feeding and water dishes, not to mention a comb and brush for last-minute touch-ups.

*

Take your cat's own litter tray. Most shows will provide the litter itself.

*

You will be assigned a cage at the show. Most people like to fix up their cages; some go into interior decorating with the abandon of a stage designer and win prizes for it, too. Some owners even build furniture in the cages, although such extravagance isn't necessary.

*

But whether or not you go in for Louis XIV décor or garden-variety chintz, you will want to hang some curtains inside. In purchasing curtain material to take along, try to complement your cat's eyes or coat—anything from red velvet to pale-blue organza to fake leopard will do. Curtains have a practical function, too, shielding your pet from distractions.

*

You will also want to take a piece of carpeting to cover the floor and top of the cage.

*

Everything should be harmonious and, like the curtains, should not clash with Tabby's coloring.

Show Day Has Arrived

Before being assigned to its cage, the doctor will give your cat a going-over as thorough as an examination at the Mayo Clinic.

*

If Tabby has never been in a show before, she may suddenly throw a fit of temperament. All those lights and strange smells are enough to turn a purring puss into a tiger in no time at all.

*

If you have an unaltered male, don't get next to another male. Result: instant uproar.

*

If your cat carries on, don't panic. It will either calm down with soft talk or it will let you know that it is not the show-biz type. If your cat continues to be obstreperous, take it home and try again. No use trying for a ribbon if all Tabby wants is a chunk of somebody's arm.

*

When the time comes for you to be "onstage," your cat will be called by a number.

*

Take your cat and place it in the judging cage with its number on top.

*

Anonymity is the order of the show, so it is important that you not talk to the judge. He or she does not want to associate any cat with any owner, no matter how fascinating either you or your cat may be.

*

The judge will score your cat on points, and at the end will announce the winners.

*

The scoring depends on the breed. A Burmese, for example, is judged on its head, eyes, muzzle, color, back, tail, legs, coat, chest, body, and feet, with major faults being body markings such as tabby marks, and white patches and the wrong eye color. Blue eyes will disqualify a Burmese.

*

Household pets, on the other hand, are judged for disposition, grooming, beauty, and condition.

*

Most shows have lots of prizes; so many, in fact, that it behooves an observer to wonder not who won, but who lost.

There are the ribbons: blue for first in class, red for second, yellow for third, and green for fourth.

A household cat can win Best Household Pet, Most Interestingly Marked Cat, Longest-tail Cat, Smartest Cat, Best-groomed cat, Greatest Actor, Best Show-Cat, etc.

Why not enter your Tabby or Felix? What can you lose? You'll be surprised at the fun you'll have and the cats you'll see, to say nothing of the friends you'll make.

Tabby and Felix will grow to love the whole scene, and you might even come home with a prize for the best cat in the world. Yours!

CHAPTER TWO

Health, Good Living and Illness

Ears

Children can hear about twenty-thousand cycles per second. Many people over sixty cannot hear frequencies above eight-thousand cycles per second. A chimpanzee does better than man, with thirty-thousand cycles per second. But the cat? Sixty-thousand cycles per second!

The most persistent and ornery ear problem of cats is undoubtedly *ear mites*. The mite lives its entire life cycle on the inner surface of the ear tissue, depositing its eggs in the nooks and crannies.

If your cat is shaking its head or pawing at its ears, take a good look inside. Mites are the answer if you notice black, brown or gray waxy material instead of the usual clean pink surface.

If mite infestation is detected, better let your vet clean out the mess with a miticide that will kill both adult mites and eggs. The doctor will then give you medication to apply at home for several days, or as long as symptoms persist.

Some of the mite medication should also be applied to the cat's tail. Cats often sleep with their tails curled around their bodies, and the tip of the tail next to their ears. Block that circle, or the tail will reinfect the ears.

In severe cases, other parts of the body should also be treated with the miticide: rear feet, and around the head and neck, but not all at once, or cat may get sick from licking the medicine.

To avoid ear problems, owners should regularly examine their cats' ears. A healthy ear is pink, dry, free of scales or scabs, swellings, or parasites.

To clean a cat's ears of wax or soil, gently wipe out the ear canal with a cotton swab moistened with a little mineral oil. Or wrap a soft washcloth around your finger.

Never probe deeply into your cat's ears. You can do more damage than good. Never go farther with any object than your finger could—and then *very* gently.

Placing the cat on a table is often an easy way to control its movements, but put a bath mat or small rug under it so it can dig its claws in.

Lap restraint is also practical if the cat is used to being held.

Infections of the ear flap are often caused by the cat scratching at fleas and raising an abscess. Cat fights also cause ear abscesses. There's nothing to do but take Puss to the animal hospital for treatment. Don't wait—abscesses are common and not dangerous, but if untreated can cause other problems, such as general infections. Also, they are uncomfortable to Puss.

Sometimes a cat will scratch or injure the skin of the ear pinna (flap) and cause blood to collect in the area. This is called a hematoma. Veterinary care is imperative to drain off the blood; otherwise, scarring and crinkling may result.

Inflammation of the inner ear can be very serious. The cat will show loss of equilibrium, head tilting, and may even fall over. Because the disease can also affect the brain, it is important that the cat be treated professionally at once.

Antibiotics and cortisone therapy are frequently used in diseases of the inner ear, but they are not always successful. This illness can be fatal.

White cats are susceptible to cancers at the tips of their ears, especially if exposed to bright sun or very low temperatures. If the ears look red, sore, and inflamed, and if they don't heal spontaneously in a short time, see a veterinarian.

If caught early enough, ear-tip cancers can be treated surgically.

Some owners of white cats routinely touch up their cats' ears with suntan lotion on bright days and keep them indoors when temperatures drop.

Eyes

We are not sure whether cats see in daylight as much as we do, less, or more. Personally, I vote for more. Ever watch a cat bat at a bug invisible to everyone else?

A cat has a very wide field of vision—about 280 degrees. A dog's field is only about 83 degrees.

It used to be gospel that cats were color-blind. Some authorities still contend it is so, but I. Weigel, in Grzimek's *Animal Life Encyclopedia,* says: "... the field retina contains rods and cones, indicating that felines have color vision." Any cat owner can prove this by offering the family cat green or purple food.

Cats have a third eyelid (called a nictitating membrane or haw) usually out of sight. Its function is to remove dust or other irritants from the eye, and possibly to protect the eye during hunting or such dangerous pursuits as eyeballing the cat next door, which has dared to set foot on home territory.

If the third eyelid half covers the eye, it is a sign of illness, generally intestinal in origin. A veterinarian should be consulted.

*

Diseases of the eye are not too common, though abrasions and lacerations from cat fights can occur, and demand veterinary attention.

Conjunctivitis (inflammation of the mucous membrane covering the anterior portion of the eye) can occur, sometimes as a result of bacterial or viral infections.

Constant discharge from the eye is a symptom of either local infection or systemic disease. Many ocular problems in cats, especially mucus discharge, are signs of serious viral diseases such as Feline Infectious Peritonitis (FIP), Feline Pneumonitis (FPN), or Feline Reovirus Infection. (See "Feline Respiratory Problems.")

If the eyeball bulges, it may be a postorbital abscess. Surgical drainage is imperative. Or it may indicate glaucoma or a tumor. If it is a tumor, it is almost always malignant and fatal.

Cats can also have cataracts, caused by trauma, progressive retinal atrophy, diabetes, or old age. Many—not all—of these cataracts can be treated by surgery. Cataracts in kittens are frequently absorbed. Only a veterinarian can tell which cataracts can be treated.

Nose

Cats can smell better than human beings, but not as well as dogs. We have about five million to twenty million olfactory cells. Dogs have between one-hundred million and three-hundred million. Cats are in between, with an estimated sixty-seven million olfactory cells.

Behind a cat's hard palate is a peripheral olfactory organ. This is a blind pouch which leads to nasal and oral cavities by means of a duct just behind the incisor teeth. Ever see a cat concentrate on an odor by extending its neck and opening its mouth slightly? Puss looks a little silly, but apparently this pose concentrates the scent by drawing it directly into the duct behind the teeth to the peripheral organ. This grimace is called *flehmen*. Ruminants and horses also go through this odd behavior. It is more prominent in them because their upper lips really curl.

Male cats often make this response to a female to determine better if she is in heat. I have also observed it often in my neutered cats when they are outdoors and detect an unfamiliar odor of urine from a passing cat. It looks as though they are repelled by it. The opposite may be true.

Cats mark their territory by scent (as do many other mammals), through spraying. Cats also scratch on trees, leaving foot gland secretions, and rub their heads and cheeks against objects, which involve the glands at the corners of the cheek or those between the eye and ear.

The Cat's Purr

Theories abound as to how a cat purrs. No one seems to know for sure. One authority swore it was merely the vibration of the soft palate. Another suggested that the purr did not originate in the throat or voice box, but in the chest, caused by an increase of activity in major blood vessels there. The most likely explanation is that the purr originates in the cat's "false" or upper vocal cords. Cats have two sets of vocal cords: false or upper; true or lower. Catty speech such as maiows come from the true.

Some—not all—of the big cats purr, too. Cats are divided into three genera: *Acinonyx, Felis,* and *Panthera.* Of the first genus, cheetahs purr. Of the *Felis* genus, the lynx, mountain lion, leopard cat, ocelot, and jaguarandi purr. There may be others, but they have not been reported. The *Panthera* (lions, leopards, panthers, jaguars, tigers) do not purr.

Cats do not seem to purr to each other except as part of the communication between Mama Cat and her kittens. It is strongly suspected that kittens find their mother's teats after birth by feeling the vibration of her purr and homing in to nourishment. Inasmuch as they are born both blind and deaf, the theory makes sense. Since kittens also purr when nursing, it may be assumed that purring is part of their instinctual responses.

Older cats purr easily on being touched or stroked or when lying on or close to their favorite human beings. I have never noted that a cat purred when in contact with another cat, no matter how friendly. And never when asleep.

Teeth

A cat has twenty-six deciduous (baby) teeth and thirty permanent teeth—sixteen above, fourteen below.

*

The baby teeth appear between two and three weeks of age, and begin to be pushed out by the permanent teeth between fourteen and sixteen weeks of age. By six months, all the permanent teeth should be in.

*

Sometimes a baby tooth is retained instead of shed. When this happens, it must be extracted, or Puss may have pain and discomfort as well as a crooked smile.

*

Cats have many of the same dental problems we do, and their teeth and gums should be examined every year. The most common problem is accumulation of tartar. This occurs most often in older cats, but can occur at any age. The veterinarian will clean off the tartar, probably under sedation. If not removed, tartar can dig into the gums, causing gingivitis and periodontitis, as well as inflammation of the tongue.

*

In severe cases of gingivitis, the gums become infected and the breath will become foul.

*

Following hospital treatment of teeth and gums, your vet may prescribe antibiotics and B-complex vitamins. He or she may also instruct you in how to apply an antiseptic solution to the infected gums (without getting nipped in the process).

*

A little dry food in the diet has proved to be a preventive in tartar build-up. However, an annual dental check-up is still necessary, especially in older cats.

*

Occasionally a tooth may abscess, causing not only pain but fever and loss of appetite. Prompt veterinary attention is imperative. Surgery will be necessary, as well as antibiotic treatment of the infection.

*

Cavities are seldom seen in cats, but once in a while they occur. If owners want to pay for it, the cavity can be filled and the tooth saved. In most instances, however, the tooth is pulled.

Cats do very well on less than their normal number of teeth. Some indoor cats live out their elderly days with no teeth at all, and do just fine.

*

Loose or broken teeth are generally extracted. However, one Persian made the news when it was outfitted with an 18-carat gold crown on one of its damaged teeth. (That was before the current gold rush, natch.)

Polydactylism

Some cats are born with more toes on each foot than the normal five up front and four in back.

*

This abnormality is more often seen on the front feet alone, but it is not uncommon to see it on all four.

*

The commonest number of toes in polydactylism is six, though some felines have as many as seven.

*

The front paws of polydactyls are often more rounded than usual, giving them a wide-track look. Owners like to call them Mittens or Big Foot.

*

The condition is hereditary, is not rare, and can be found all over the country, contrary to the belief held by some New Englanders, who like to think it is a specialty of their region, where eccentricities are often admired.

*

Polydactylism is found in both sexes and in all kinds of cats. Its gene seems to bring no other characteristics with it, either lethal or beneficial.

*

Owners are often proud of their cats' many toes, and think the trait gives them a distinctive look. It does. A clumsy one.

*

If the trait is found in a purebred, however, it is disqualified from cat shows.

Constipation

Most cats have one or two bowel movements a day. A few maintain good health on a much less frequent schedule. There is no cause for alarm unless the cat shows signs of illness, such as listlessness or loss of appetite or any other behavioral change. If the stool is very dry and hard, as well as infrequent, some corrective measures should be taken.

*

Raw liver is a natural laxative. If the cat likes it, a small serving, no more often than twice a week, may do the trick.

*

Milk is also laxative to many cats. If your Felix is showing signs of constipation, you might try adding a *little* milk to his food.

*

Do not give him Vaseline (sometimes erroneously suggested) or any other mineral oil, because prolonged use prevents absorption of one of the B vitamins.

*

A special laxative for cats can be purchased at most pet stores. One such product is called Petromalt. There are others of a similar nature. All are perfectly okay for cats.

Diarrhea

Of all ailments affecting our pet cats, diarrhea is among the most common and the most messy.

*

A simple change of diet may be the only offender, and can be easily tested by reverting to the original diet.

*

Milk causes diarrhea in many cats.

*

The same holds true of raw liver. *Cooked* liver works in the opposite way.

*

Other causes of diarrhea include mere nervousness, allergy to food, poisons, parasites, or improper absorption of food. Fecal analysis may be needed to determine the exact cause.

*

If the problem is a suspected food allergy, an elimination diet is a good way to find out *if* and *which*. Feed Miss Puss nothing but parboiled lamb (ground) mixed with cooked rice twice a day for three or four days. Offer distilled water only. If diarrhea stops, the answer is undoubtedly a food. Add a new food every three days and watch the stool. If diarrhea recurs, the last food added is the culprit.

Worms

If your cat appears malnourished even though you know you have been feeding it well, has frequent loose stools, a lackluster coat, and a bloated stomach, you should suspect worms.

Worms come in several varieties: roundworms, tapeworms, stomach-worms, hookworms, whipworms, and threadworms. They all live in a cat's gastrointestinal tract, and the eggs are excreted in bowel movements (but not in every one).

It is not as important for the layman to be able to differentiate between all the types of parasites as it is for the cat owner to take the cat to a veterinarian for fecal analysis if worms are suspected from either observation of fecal material or your cat's general health.

Follow the doctor's treatment procedures if worms are found. Don't go ahead on your own and worm your cat with a product you've seen advertised. All worming medications can be dangerous if used incorrectly.

Cats can become infected with worms at any age, but kittens are especially susceptible.

Restricting your cat's hunting, eliminating fleas that can carry tapeworms, and washing litter pans every day, are all things you can do to prevent worms. You must be very careful, even if your cat is indoors most or all of the time.

Two other types of worms—flukes, which locate in the liver and lungs, and lungworms, which cause severe coughing—are far less common than the varieties mentioned above. Treatment of both is difficult and not very satisfactory.

When a cat scoots along the floor dragging its rear end, the problem is *not* always worms but impaction of the anal glands. These sacs are located just inside the anus, and are normally emptied during bowel movements. Occasionally they become impacted, however, and then veterinary attention is necessary.

Vomiting

A cat goes into reverse gear very easily. If your Tabby throws up during eating, it may be nothing more than a hair in her throat or too big a mouthful of food. If she vomits after eating, it could be worms, hairballs, or constipation. An examination of the vomitus or stool by a veterinarian should be helpful in indicating which it is.

To keep your cats free of hairballs, groom them regularly. Brush short-haired cats every day; comb long-haired cats. During shedding season, give them weekly doses of Petromalt or similar medication, obtainable at most pet stores.

Coughing and choking and/or vomiting can also be caused by a congenital kink in the esophagus called an achalasia. Your vet can also help you with this. Surgery is sometimes performed, but feeding several small meals a day rather than two larger ones will often control the problem.

If your cat coughs or chokes a great deal, take it to the vet. It may be suffering from allergies to pollen, dust, feathers, or wool—or perhaps only to a stressful situation in the household. Jealousy, believe it or not, can bring on an asthmatic attack.

Allergies are treated by medication (corticosteroids) and by eliminating the offending element in the environment, if possible.

The only other reason for frequent vomiting is illness. Tabby may be suffering from an infection, bowel obstruction, or something worse. If your cat vomits and then refuses to eat for more than a day or exhibits other signs of malaise such as diarrhea, take her to the vet immediately.

Inoculations

All cats must have inoculations against three very dangerous diseases:
1. Panleukopenia (also called feline infectious enteritis, and mistakenly named feline distemper).
2. Rhinotracheitis (FVR); *and*
3. Calicivirus, which together account for about 80 percent of all upper-respiratory diseases of cats and which take a combined vaccine, either by injection or intranasally.

Also important for cats who go outdoors:
1. Rabies vaccination. Cats have to be bitten by a rabid animal to be infected, but skunks, bats, and foxes—not to mention an occasional stray dog—are all hazards.
2. Pneumonitis (Chlamydia) inoculation is also recommended.

None of the vaccines is recommended for pregnant cats.

Here is the timing for a comprehensive vaccination program for cats (according to Charles Povey, BVSc., Ph.D., MRCVS, as published in *Feline Practice*, September 1977).

Age	Vaccines
6 weeks	FVR + Calici
9 to 12 weeks	FVR + Calici + Panleukopenia
12 weeks	Pneumonitis (Chlamydia)
16 weeks	Rabies
9 months	FVR + Calici
15 months and annually	FVR + Calici + Panleukopenia + Pneumonitis + Rabies (divided between 2 appointments)

For further details, see the sections on Panleukopenia and Feline Respiratory Diseases.

The Great Cat Killer

It is commonly called distemper. But its real name is *feline infectious enteritis,* or *panleukopenia.* It is also called cat fever, cat plague, and agranulocytosis.

By any name, this disease is very serious, and claims the lives of up to 90 percent of those cats unlucky enough to contract it. Indeed, it ranks second only to the automobile as a cause of death to felines.

It has been labeled "the great cat killer."

*

It's hard to believe, but relatively few cats are immunized against this dread disease, despite the fact that veterinarians have a vaccine that is remarkably effective against it.

*

Many cat owners seem to be unaware of this potential killer. Some confuse the name with dog distemper and further confuse that with erratic behavior and foaming at the mouth. Some dogs with distemper may manifest such wild actions, but foaming at the mouth is much more common in dogs with rabies. Since cats are much less apt to get rabies, owners overlook the possibility of what cats *do* get.

*

The dog, horse, mink, fox, and ferret are all subject to diseases called distemper. Aside from mink, none of them has any relation whatever to feline distemper, nor can they be transmitted from any one species to any other.

*

The raccoon is the only species outside the cat family (the disease can strike *all* cats) known to be susceptible to it.

*

The cause of the disease is a virus (panleukopenia) which attacks the white blood cells, causing a critical drop in count (at the height of the disease, from a normal fifteen thousand white cells per cubic centimeter to two thousand). The bacteria in the lower intestinal tract rage unchecked.

*

Although this disease can strike cats of any age, it is most common in cats under two years of age, and particularly in kittens.

*

It strikes so suddenly that many owners think their pets have been poisoned.

*

The disease is highly contagious and is transmitted through direct contact or through the tears, sputum, nasal discharge, feces, or urine of affected cats.

*

Even after affected cats have been placed in isolation, the danger persists, as the virus can live outside the cat's body for two weeks, and even longer under the right conditions.

What Are the Symptoms?

The symptoms of panleukopenia are weakness, fever, and loss of appetite.

*

Anyone who has ever seen a cat in the throes of the disease cannot escape the memory of his or her pet standing over its food or water dish as though wanting to eat or drink, but being too weak to be able to do so. Some cats have been known to crave sitting in a sink next to a running faucet, though they can't even open their mouths to drink.

*

Often a cat vomits, first food, then bile. Diarrhea may occur immediately or a day or so after the onset of illness. The skin and coat become dry due to dehydration. Erosion in the mouth may cause a bad odor.

*

The cat grows weaker by the hour, until it can't move.

What Can the Veterinarian Do?

Confronted with a case of distemper, the doctor tries to fight the dehydration, deadly in itself, by getting liquid into the cat intravenously. He or she tries to give nourishment in the same way. Veterinarians will administer antibiotics. They'll try to check the diarrhea, the vomiting. They'll use serums and vaccines. Then they'll cross their fingers.

*

Most veterinarians agree that the odds against them are very long when it comes to curing a case of panleukopenia. It is often fatal, despite everything one tries to do.

*

Sometimes the cat will seem better, then sink back again. That's why veterinarians insist that their patients remain in the hospital at least a couple of days after an apparent recovery.

*

Curiously, cats who recover seldom show any aftereffects, but they can be carriers for as long as three months.

What Is the Answer?

Veterinarians agree completely: vaccination ensures almost *100 percent immunity*.

*

In no other area of veterinary medicine are there more effective vaccines. Most kittens should be vaccinated at nine to twelve weeks, with a second shot two or three weeks later. Or one shot may be given at nine to twelve weeks, depending on the vaccine.

*

Booster shots should be given annually throughout the cat's life.

*

A kitten usually receives immunity from its mother's milk while it's nursing, provided, of course, that Mama was vaccinated before becoming pregnant.

*

However your family comes by kittens, from your own mother cat or from a neighbor's, make sure yours receives its inoculations—and on time!

Cancer

Because cancer in any one of its various forms is among the foremost killers of cats, owners should be aware of symptoms.

*

Approximately 75 percent of tumors in cats turn out to be malignant. Any suspicious lump should be promptly examined by a veterinarian. Many tumors, if caught early enough, can be treated with either surgery or radiation.

*

Bone cancer in cats is almost always fatal. The first symptoms are usually lameness and/or a swelling on the bone. X-rays will determine if the disease is cancer or merely arthritis or an injury. Prognosis is poor because of the speed with which it spreads to the lungs and other organs.

*

A cat's mouth should be examined regularly for possible tumors, as cancer of the mouth is common. Even a small ulcer should be treated by a veterinarian; it could be the beginning of a malignant tumor. Many such tumors can be removed surgically if caught in early stages. If allowed to spread, they can involve the nose or jaw.

*

Skin cancers are especially amenable to treatment by surgery, and the rate of cure is high. If the malignancy has spread to other parts of the body, however, it is probably too late.

*

Female cats that have not been spayed have a greater chance of developing mammary cancer than spayed cats. Older females are more susceptible than young females. Breast tumors spread rapidly. Some are treatable by surgery.

Leukemia:

The most common feline malignancy is leukemia. It is, in fact, much more common in cats than in either dogs or humans.

Feline leukemia is not one disease but a complex of several diseases caused by a virus located mostly in bone marrow, lymph nodes, spleen, and salivary glands. These diseases include disorders of the blood cells, as well as lymphosarcoma. (Some lymphosarcomas are *not* associated with feline leukemia.)

The symptoms of the feline leukemia virus (FeLV) in a cat vary enormously. If the cat has the lymphosarcoma type it may first only seem depressed, lethargic, and not interested in food. Other cats may exhibit difficulty in breathing, indicating the tumor has invaded the chest. Still others may vomit or become emaciated and show marked loss in weight.

If the cat has the classic type of leukemia, its first symptoms will be paleness of gums, nose, and mucous membranes. The cat will appear listless and weak.

Diagnosis of a feline-leukemia-virus-related disease depends on blood tests as well as a special immunofluorescent test for FeLV. Other tests for kidney and liver function may be required, as well as examination of the bone marrow.

A cat can register positive for FeLV and still display no signs of illness. The cat may stay healthy all its life, but there is a good chance it will communicate the disease to other cats in a multi-cat household. Isolation is therefore imperative.

A negative FeLV test result doesn't rule out the possibility that the cat has lymphosarcoma. Other tests will have to be used.

Cats with only FeLV may develop lymphosarcoma at some later age. Lymphosarcoma is considered untreatable and fatal, though chemotherapy sometimes prolongs life a short while.

*

Cats with leukemia often perk up with blood transfusions, cortisone therapy, and doses of testosterone, vitamins, and minerals, but eventually will probably succumb to it.

*

Feline leukemia is *not* contagious to man.

*

If an infected cat is taken out of a family, do not bring a new cat into the house until three months have passed.

*

GOOD NEWS: In March of 1980, a vaccine which prevents the onset of feline leukemia, but is not effective after contraction of the disease, was developed by veterinary researchers at Ohio State University. We can look forward to its being available to the public in a year or so, possibly less.

Feline Infectious Peritonitis (FIP)

Feline Infectious Peritonitis (FIP) is one of several viral diseases of cats, in a group that includes panleukopenia, respiratory infections, and leukemia. The first successful isolation of the FIP virus in cell cultures was not accomplished until 1978, though the disease has been known since the early sixties.

*

The virus (a coronavirus) infects either the intestinal or respiratory tract. A diagnosis of FIP should be taken very seriously by any cat owner.

*

Symptoms of FIP range from mild to severe. Primary indications may be merely fever, bronchitis, and runny eyes. This is sometimes called the *dry* variety. In the secondary stages, a more generalized infection pervades the body, affecting many organs, particularly the liver, and often resulting in a build-up of fluid in the abdomen and/or chest. The central nervous system may also be involved. This is often called the *wet* FIP.

*

Transmission of the FIP virus from cat to cat is thought to be through the respiratory system, urine, and feces. Pregnant female cats may also transmit the disease to their unborn kittens, causing abortions, stillbirths, and endometritis (inflammation of the lining of the uterus) in the queens.

46

Treatment of either dry or wet FIP is generally futile, though some drugs are being tried, with only a minimal cure rate. Nearly half of the cats with FIP are also positive for feline leukemia virus (FeLV).

*

There is no vaccine available against FIP.

*

FIP is not contagious to man.

Diabetes

Cats can get most of the diseases human beings are susceptible to, plus a few of their own. One serious ailment common to people and cats (also dogs) is diabetes. If your cat starts losing weight at the same time it drinks and urinates to excess, and eats as though there were no tomorrow, chances are good that it has diabetes.

*

An examination by a veterinarian of the cat's blood and urine can determine a diabetes diagnosis—which means, of course, a malfunctioning pancreas.

*

Treatment of diabetes in cats is like that in humans: daily injections of insulin and diet control. Medication by mouth has not been successful with either cats or dogs.

Epilepsy

Epilepsy is more common in cats than is generally realized. Symptoms are seizures or "fits," during which the cat twitches, writhes, sometimes flies through the air to land on the floor, and often loses bladder control. The cat then wakes up as though nothing has happened. The episode is over for the moment.

*

Some authorities believe thiamine deficiency may contribute to seizures, but whatever the cause, epilepsy in cats can be controlled by anticonvulsant drugs.

*

If your cat shows signs of seizures, take it to your veterinarian for tests and treatment. The doctor will teach you how to give your cat its medication at home. Chances are good Puss can live out its life quite happy and symptom-free.

47

Heart Disease

It was thought for years that, except for aortic thromboembolism, cats seldom suffered from heart disease. Now we know they can and do. They can be born with heart problems or they can acquire them. To evaluate a cat with possible heart disease, complete history must be taken and a physical examination, as well as radiographic and electrocardiographic studies, must be made.

*

If your cat shows signs of difficulty in breathing or abdominal distention, heart disease may be suspected.

*

Acquired heart disease usually involves the heart muscle (as opposed to the valves in congenital heart conditions), and must be treated by a veterinarian in the hospital, at least at first. Therapy can then be continued at home. Rest, slowing of the heart rate, improvement of cardiac efficiency, drugs to relieve congestion and edema are weapons in the arsenal, depending on the type of problem.

*

If you notice posterior paralysis, coldness of the hind legs, and an absence of femoral pulses in your cat, it could be aortic thromboembolism. Surgery is sometimes successful if the problem is detected early enough.

High-Rise Syndrome (HRS)

Veterinarians in big cities are reporting an increase in High Rise Syndrome (HRS) among cats. In cities like New York, cats live all their lives in apartments, and like to sit on window sills basking in the sun and watching the passing parade. If the window is left open, or if the cat has access to a terrace, it sometimes loses its balance and heads for the pavement.

*

Although cats can right themselves with amazing grace, they can also be killed or maimed as a result of a long dive. The ASPCA in New York City treats more than 150 cases of HRS a year.

*

The record distance cats have fallen and survived, according to the magazine *Off-Lead,* is eighteen stories onto a hard surface, twenty stories onto shrubbery, and twenty-eight stories onto a canopy or awning. If you have a cat in a high-rise apartment, don't try to break the record. You will only break the cat.

Feline Respiratory Problems

The "common cold" is a complicated feline ailment that all cat owners should know more about and many will have to deal with. Thanks to research funded by the Morris Animal Foundation and work by various drug companies, the types of respiratory infection in cats have been sorted out and vaccines created to immunize them against three of the most common respiratory ailments.

All four types of respiratory infections are highly contagious. Furthermore, cats can and do die from respiratory diseases. For both reasons, it is important that pet owners be aware of the discernible differences in symptoms among the various types of respiratory ailments. Important, too, is knowledge of the vaccines now on the market to insure your cat's good health.

Feline Viral Rhinotracheitis (FVR).

This is a herpes virus infection and one of the two most common respiratory diseases that affect the cat. It accounts for about 45 percent of the total number and can be *very* serious. (A cat's nasal passages are unusually complicated, and that fact accounts for part of the difficulty.)

Symptoms: sneezing, coughing, fever, redness and dripping of the eyes and nose, drooling, mouth breathing, loss of appetite.

In pregnant cats, FVR can cause abortion or stillbirth.

Feline Caliciviral Disease (FCD).

This is as common as FVR, and in its severe form can cause pneumonia with obvious labored breathing and "rattles."

There is a high incidence of such severe types of infection in kittens. Often, however, it is seen only in its mild form.

Symptoms: ulceration of the mouth (especially the tongue), hard palate and/or nostrils, occasional fever, loss of appetite, depression. Sneezing and coughing are not characteristic.

Feline Pneumonitis (FPN).

This is a term used to cover all respiratory infections that affect the cat.

Today the name refers only to the one we now know is caused by *Chlamydia psittaci,* a feline strain of a bacterialike bug that causes psittacosis in birds.

*

It is present in relatively few cases—and those, fairly mild—of respiratory infections (only 5 to 10 percent).

*

Symptoms: Conjunctivitis in one or both eyes with a lot of discharge. The third eyelid will sometimes be swollen. There may or may not be sneezing and fever. Rarely does the cat stop eating, though its appetite may not be as perky as usual.

*

A characteristic of this Chlamydia infection is that cats seem to recover, then relapse with recurrent episodes of conjunctivitis.

*

On rare occasions, the owner of the cat may be infected with Chlamydia conjunctivitis from his or her cat.

Feline Reovirus Infection.

Commonly called Reo, it is the mildest of all the respiratory diseases of cats. An animal can appear little affected beyond a clear discharge from its eyes and an aversion to light.

*

No fever or loss of appetite is generally noted. The nose and mouth are not involved.

Immunizations Available:

Of the four disease types discussed, there are effective vaccines for the first three. Reo virus is so mild that no vaccine has been developed. Because of the possible severity and contagiousness of the first three, however, a program of regular vaccination can now be undertaken with excellent prophylactic results.

*

Excellent studies have been made comparing the intramuscular (IM) or subcutaneous (SC) types of vaccines for the first two respiratory infections to the newer intranasal vaccine (in the form of drops) developed by Norden against both FDR and FCD. Results indicate that the intranasal vaccination gives a more complete protection but at the expense of "shedding" (mild sneezing, nasal discharge, mouth ulcer, and conjunctivitis) afterward. This could, of course, endanger nonvaccinated cats in the same household or cattery, but doesn't hurt the vaccinated cat and only lasts a few days.

*

There is no "shedding" from the IM or SC varieties.

*

As for duration of the intranasal vaccine protection, one dose, followed by annual boosters, seems to be enough.

*

If you as a pet owner prefer the intramuscular or subcutaneous types of vaccines for your cat, either one is safe and effective.

*

Six-month or annual booster shots are advised, depending on the brand administered. Let your veterinarian decide.

*

Don't fail to vaccinate your cat against respiratory infections. Preferably do it when your cat is young. If that time is past, do it *now*.

*

Consult your veterinarian as to *which* vaccine, and *when*.

Comprehensive Vaccination Program for Respiratory Ailments for Cats★

Age	*Vaccines (IM) or (SC)*†
6 weeks	FVR + Calici
9 to 12 weeks	FVR + Calici
12 weeks	Chlamydia (Pneumonitis)
9 months	FVR + Calici
15 months, then annually	FVR + Calici + Chlamydia (divided between two appointments)

Pneumonia

Cats exposed to long periods of cold and rain or snow sometimes come down with pneumonia, just as people do. It can also occur as a complication of other respiratory diseases.

★ Derived from an article by Charles Povey, B.V.Sc., Ph.D., M.R.C.V.S., Department of Clinical Studies of Ontario Veterinary College in Guelph, Canada, in *Feline Practice*, September 1977.

† See section on "Inoculations."

Bacterial pneumonia is a very serious disease. Its symptoms include high fever, difficult breathing, anorexia, and often, collapse. If you put your ear against the cat's chest you can hear a definite wheeze or rasp.

If you suspect your cat has pneumonia, get it to the vet immediately. A cat with pneumonia may be too sick to treat at home; only your doctor can advise you. Wherever it is, the cat will need regular dosing with antibiotics and a warm, dry place to rest. If you can care for your cat at home, all the better. But if antibiotic injections are needed, the hospital may be the only choice.

Sinus Trouble

Cats sometimes contract sinusitis as a sequel to a respiratory infection. The symptoms include sneezing and nasal discharge, such as occur in the "common cold."

It is a condition sometimes hard to treat because of the difficulty of getting medication to the area. The blood supply to the sinus cavity does not permit easy access for giving the necessary antibiotics.

If the condition does not clear up even after culture and sensitivity tests have been done and appropriate medication administered, it is often necessary to open up the sinus cavity and irrigate it regularly with antibiotics and enzymes to fight the infection and expel the debris.

Skin Problems

Cats have beautiful fur—when they're healthy—but they are also susceptible to all kinds of annoying skin problems.

Hair coat:

Because hair is almost 100 percent protein, any decrease in protein intake can cause your cat's coat to look ratty. A long illness, for instance, always shows up in a dry, dull coat and shedding all over the house.

Also, under any prolonged stress such as pregnancy or lactation, the hair will fall out in what seems like excessive amounts. It will, however, grow back.

The two heavy shedding periods for cats and dogs are spring, when the number of light hours increases, and fall, when it decreases. If your cat lives indoors all the time it will shed all year long because the light does not vary that much between seasons.

Feline Acne:

Some cats suffer from pimples on the chin and lower lip, possibly owing to overactive sebaceous glands or to incomplete cleaning procedures. Whatever the cause, the condition is unsightly and must be treated professionally by a veterinarian or abscesses may occur. The doctor will clean out the pimples, and then prescribe antibiotics. The condition frequently recurs, but is not contagious.

Ringworm:

The most contagious feline skin disease is ringworm, which is *not* caused by a worm, but by a superficial fungus. It shows up as one or several well-marked areas of hair loss, scaling, and irritation, especially on the legs and head. It doesn't seem to cause itching, but can spread not only to other animals, but to people. Treatment by a vet consists of applying ointment locally and giving Griseofulvin by mouth. Care must also be taken to protect other animals and humans in the cat's household.

Notoedric Mange:

This is a parasitic disease caused by mites easily seen under a microscope. It affects a cat's head with an unsightly thick, yellow crust resulting in hair loss from the ears. If it's not checked, it spreads to the face and down the back. It is very itchy and very contagious.

Otodectic Mange:

This is another name for ear mites, discussed elsewhere in this book. This condition is much more common than Notoedric Mange.

Demodectic Mange:

Sometimes called "red mange," this disease is less common than the above in cats, though often found in dogs. It usually affects only young cats, and is found on the face or forelegs as a small bold red spot that spreads. It is very itchy.

All three types of mange must be treated by a veterinarian.

Flea Dermatitis:

This is the most common parasitic disease of cats, appearing as little red crusty bumps that become open sores when the cat scratches them open. This disease is easy to diagnose, but hard to cure. (See "Fleas.")

Eosinophilic Granuloma:

Sometimes this is called "rodent ulcer," and appears on the upper lip, typified by large areas of slightly raised lesions with red ulcerated surfaces. The condition is thought to be allergic in origin and sometimes responds to Ovaban, though it frequently recurs.

Linear Granuloma:

Cousin to the above, this affects the hind legs and the side of the chest.

Neurodermatitis:

This is a disease authorities know little about. The cat suddenly starts pulling out its hair, frequently from the chest. No physical cause seems to be present, but psychological trauma such as a new pet or baby in the household is suspected.

Solar Dermatitis:

In California, Arizona, or other areas where there is a lot of sunshine, white cats sometimes have problems with their ears. (See "Ears.") They become red and scaly and begin to lose hair along the edges. If not treated, skin cancer can develop. The cat may also have to be kept indoors during the sunniest hours of the day.

Urinary Problems (Feline Urologic Syndrome—FUS)

One of the most common feline health problems—especially in male cats— is infection or blockage of the urinary tract. This is called Feline Urologic Syndrome (FUS) and covers many conditions, from cystitis and urethritis to urethral obstruction.

Because of the smaller urethral opening, this problem occurs predominantly in male cats, though it is occasionally also found in females.

Symptoms of FUS include: sudden disturbance in toilet habits (the cat urinates on the rug, in the bathtub, or any place but his litter pan), frequent urination in small quantities, straining to urinate without results, blood in the urine, excessive thirst, listlessness, poor appetite.

*

In severe cases, blockage of the urethra by stones or sediment occurs and the cat cannot void at all. The result will be uremic poisoning, coma and death, unless emergency aid is received. Frequently this involves surgery.

*

Research at Cornell University has brought out the fact that FUS seems to be related to a virus. Other authorities add stress and diet, and still others include heredity among the causes.

*

At the first signs of FUS, rush your cat to the veterinarian. This is an emergency situation. He or she will prescribe medication and a program to prevent recurrence. This will include antibiotics, diet, water, and possibly a prophylactic therapy to alter the urine pH to create a less favorable environment for crystals. Urine must be acidic, not alkaline.

*

For years it was thought that high ash content in cat food (especially in dry food) *caused* FUS. There is no evidence to support this. In experimental studies, cats have been fed up to 30 percent ash diets and did not develop FUS.

*

However, if your cat has already suffered a bout of FUS, dry food is not recommended. For reasons not clearly understood, dry food *may* aggravate the problem in a cat already predisposed to the disease.

*

A parenthetical but important point concerns the difference in ash content between canned and dry cat food. To compare them, one must take into account the large difference in water content of the two products. For instance, a canned product may contain 74 percent water and a dry product, 10 percent water. If the ash content of the canned product is listed as 4 percent and of the dry as 11.9 percent, *on a moisture-free basis* this translates to 15 percent ash content for canned and 13 percent for dry food.

*

Some ash in a cat food is important. It contributes calcium, phosphorus, sodium, potassium, iron, copper, and other essential nutrients.

A diet to counteract stress and a predisposition to FUS should be high in protein and fat.

*

Some veterinarians recommend a serving of fresh raw liver, kidney, and heart two or three times weekly as a protein supplement.

*

If a cat has shown a predisposition to FUS, it must be encouraged to drink more water. You can try sprinkling a little salt on its food to stimulate thirst. Fresh water must be available at all times, especially at night.

*

Fish is generally eliminated from the diet because of its occasional high mercury content.

*

Some breeders have had good luck in preventing FUS in their catteries by adding a half teaspoon of cider vinegar to the cats' food. If a cat balks at the taste, try a drop or two at a time, gradually working up to the half teaspoon. This helps to keep the urine acidic.

*

Tomato juice has the same effect.

*

Some authorities suggest giving a vitamin C tablet a day. Check with your veterinarian for the proper dosage.

*

A clean litter pan is very important in the control of FUS. Some veterinarians believe FUS can be contracted from a soiled pan.

*

Castration has no effect on the incidence of FUS.

First Aid

For feline emergencies, keep the following in the house: a rectal thermometer, Vaseline, Unguentine or another similar commercial product, baking soda, vinegar, bandages, cotton swabs, baby aspirin.

*

If an injured cat is bleeding, stop the bleeding by applying a pressure bandage over the wound. Use a large handkerchief or towel or other clean cloth. See a veterinarian right away.

Don't attempt to clean a major wound, but try not to let more dirt get into it.

If the cat is out of control and liable to hurt you, use heavy leather gloves. Restraint in a towel, blanket, or pillowcase may also be effective. I once transported a cat in convulsions wrapped in two pillowcases and, on the advice of my veterinarian, put him in the trunk of the car in case he tried to fly about. It worked fine.

If the animal is paralyzed, don't pick it up in your arms, but make a stretcher out of a board or a blanket or coat pulled taut between two carriers.

Do not give any medication without instructions from your veterinarian.

*

If a limb appears to be broken (this often results from an auto accident), wrap it firmly (but not so tightly that it interferes with blood supply) in a towel, newspaper, or magazine as a temporary splint.

*

Call your veterinarian or emergency hospital for further instructions; time is of the essence.

In the case of small burns, apply Unguentine or some other commercial product for burns, or soak a cloth in strong tea and apply to the burned area. Ice is also recommended to reduce pain.

*

If the burn is extensive, do none of the above, but rush the cat to the vet.

*

In poisoning cases, call your vet *immediately* and do what he advises. Acid poisoning is treated with a diluted solution of baking soda in water. Alkali poisoning is treated with a diluted acidic solution such as vinegar. (See "Safety.")

*

A cat's normal temperature is between 100.4 and 101.6 degrees F.

*

A cat's normal heartbeat is from 110 to 130 beats per minute.

Cats go into shock easily after injury. Keep them warm but not hot, and call the vet immediately.

Hot-Weather Tips

Summertime, and the livin's misery for Felix. Unlike a dog, he can't let his tongue hang down to his clavicle for cooling purposes, and baby, it's hot inside that fur.

The kindest thing you can do for Felix in hot weather is to leave him alone. He knows better than you do how to handle the summer blahs.

When the temperature hits ninety degrees you can count on your cat to find the coolest spot in the house. Favorite cat coolers include bare tile floors, the basement, bathtub, or even the kitchen sink if your back is turned.

If your cat is outdoors on a hot day, it will find a shady spot under the porch or a damp corner of the garden and sack out.

*

Don't worry if Felix's appetite cools off as the temperature heats up. He's just dealing with the heat in a sensible way. If he's a kitten, though, give him small amounts of food frequently, and make sure he doesn't fast too long.

*

On hot summer days, keep checking your cat's water supply. Fresh, cool water is essential all year round, but especially during the summer months. Don't fill her bowl with water you take out of the refrigerator. Use cold water from the tap, and freshen often.

*

Grooming is essential in hot weather because cats are shedding old fur, depositing it on all the furniture. If you comb or brush your cat every day (or oftener), you will prevent it not only from ingesting quantities of hair (later to be eliminated as hairballs), but from matting.

*

Don't shave or clip a cat in the mistaken idea you are keeping it cool. Cats have been known to exhibit symptoms of severe psychological trauma when clipped.

*

If Felix keels over from heat prostration, emergency measures are needed. Place him immediately in a tub of cool water or cover him with cool, wet towels. Spray the towels to keep them cool. Check his temperature rectally. Keep the treatment up until the temperature is down to 101.5 degrees. Sometimes cold-water enemas are given, but let a vet do it. When Felix recovers, offer him cool water and small amounts of food.

*

If you are taking Felix someplace in a car, even if only a few blocks and the temperature is high, *don't*, we beg you, leave him in the car while you do a little shopping en route, *even* if you have the windows open the prescribed notch or two. Your cat may be broiled before you return. Do your shopping when he is safe at home.

Winter Dangers

Although the cat did not evolve in cold climes, it can adapt to subfreezing temperatures if it has to. Naturally, long-haired cats do better than short-haired, though even the latter grow plushier coats if exposed to cold over a period of time.

*

In winter, an outdoor cat needs more calories to "stoke" its furnace than in summer.

*

It is thought that constant extremes of temperature are not as hard on a cat—provided it has shelter from rain and wind and plenty of food—than sudden changes from hot to very cold.

The cat must be able to maintain its body temperature. If it goes below normal and stays there for a considerable period of time, it can go into a coma, or may even die.

If your cat has been exposed to severe cold so long that it appears frozen, immerse it immediately in warm water. Call your vet for further instructions. (Partial thawing is dangerous.)

Frostbite of the ears is also occasionally experienced. The skin turns white, the tips of the cat's ears may even slough off, and the hair becomes discolored. No harm is done except to the cat's vanity.

Don't let your cat drink from pools of antifreeze that often gather under cars. It is poisonous.

Grooming

Some cats have oily fur and require a bath more often than others. Daily grooming with a steel comb and the application of cornstarch when the fur becomes soiled or oily can lengthen the time between baths.

It has been estimated that cats groom themselves about a third of their waking time. Grooming is essential to a cat's health and well-being. An unkempt coat is one sign that a cat is depressed and sick. A cat will also groom itself to relieve anxiety. As Mama Cat said to her kitten in Paul Gallico's delightful, *The Silent Miaow*, "When in doubt, wash."

Types of grooming include face and ear washing, licking of body and legs, biting at the coat and tail and slicking down, pulling at the claws with the teeth. If the top of the head is soiled (often from rolling in the garden), it is sometimes washed by another cat in the household, as though it were understood this is a hard place to reach.

When a cat rubs up against chairs, doors, or other objects, apparently scratching its cheeks or chin, it is probably not grooming itself but scent-marking. There are glands in the corners of the mouth and in the supraorbital region that would suggest this.

All this getting beautiful and sleek takes not only time but a rough tongue. Most of the hair that is groomed away is probably swallowed because of the barblike, backward-projecting filiform papillae on a cat's tongue. The result is often hairballs.

Although cats ordinarily cough up hairballs regularly (especially in warm weather when shedding is greatest) or eliminate them with their stools, they can still suffer occasionally from one that will not go up or down. The signs are constipation, lack of appetite, coughing, or merely depression. A few doses of Petromalt or some other commercial product will do the trick.

In serious cases of hairball obstruction (when it is just sitting between the stomach and the lower bowel without budging), strangulation of the intestine can occur if surgery is not performed. Such cases are, luckily, rare.

The best *preventive* is regular brushing or combing.

Grooming should begin when the cat is a kitten so that it becomes accustomed to the daily ritual. The earlier you start, the better chance of having your kitten associate grooming with pleasure instead of panic.

Have on hand a good steel comb with rounded teeth, a brush, a nail clipper designed especially for cats, a chamois glove, and blunt-edged scissors.

Shorthairs are brushed and longhairs combed. When you're brushing Felix Shorthair, be sure to pay special attention to the area between his shoulders, where he cannot properly clean.

If she isn't too big, place Tabby Longhair on your lap for combing. Turn her upside down and comb with easy, gentle strokes, lifting the fur

away from the skin. Start at the area under the chin and work south, not neglecting the tail. Then turn her over and do the same for the back, going down the breeches to the feet.

*

Repeat combing several times on each side until shedding stops or is reduced to a minimum.

*

If your cat is too large for the lap routine or if it doesn't like it, put it on a table with a piece of carpeting or a rubber mat under its feet so it can get a grip on it and feel secure.

*

If you encounter matted or tangled fur, use your fingers to separate the hairs, then comb. Never yank or pull too hard. Remember how *you* hated to have your curls combed out?

*

If the matting is too bad—or if Tabby has rolled into a burr or wad of chewing gum—you may need to cut it away with blunt-edged scissors. Be careful to direct the end away from Tabby so as not to hurt her. Cut in the direction of the hair rather than across it. Or better yet, put a thin comb between the mat and skin, and cut on top of the comb.

*

After combing or brushing, use a chamois cloth to bring out the luster of the cat's coat.

*

During the grooming operation, check carefully for fleas, which can be anywhere but are especially fond of the areas around ears, face, and tail.

*

If summer has brought on an invasion of fleas, invest in a flea comb. Dip it in alcohol with each stroke and comb against the direction the hair grows. If fleas are numerous, sterner measures will have to be taken. (See "Fleas.")

*

In case you're wondering about your cat's whiskers during the grooming session, remember that they're meant to be viewed, not violated. They serve to help a cat in its sensory perceptions. Do *not* trim or clip.

*

Don't poke inside your cat's ears, which are very sensitive. While grooming, though, take a good look inside. If there's a buildup of dark wax, take a cotton swab or a washcloth wrapped around your finger and, with an application of a small amount of mineral oil or alcohol, gently wipe out the wax.

*

If, while examining Tabby's ears, you see small black specks, she may have ear mites, very uncomfortable to a cat's sensitive ears. Consult your veterinarian. (See "Ears.")

*

NEVER PROBE WITH A SHARP INSTRUMENT INSIDE ANY ANIMAL'S EARS.

*

Some very light-colored cats have more ocular discharge than others and will show eye stains. Daily wiping should prevent those brown stains which appear under the eyes.

*

If eye stains do develop, you will have to wash them thoroughly, before they get worse, with a diluted peroxide solution.

*

During primping time, examine your cat's teeth. Tartar builds up on all cats' teeth. Dry food will cut this down enormously but not remove it entirely. If it is time for a good cleaning, take your pet to a veterinarian for the job. It requires special equipment.

*

Occasionally it is a good idea to massage Tabby's gums with salt water to help reduce mouth odors and keep the bacteria growth in check.

*

Check Tabby's nails while you're grooming her. All cats should have their nails clipped about twice a month.

*

First, equip yourself with a set of nail clippers designed for cats. Inasmuch as a cat's claws are retractable, you have to press down on the base of each toe to "let out" the nail from its sheath. Don't hurry; you don't want to frighten or hurt Puss. Working over a light is helpful in seeing the tiny, thin blood vessel that runs down the center of the nail. You are going to clip the transparent end of the nail, not the quick. If you trim too closely and nick the vein you will see blood. Don't panic; hold a piece of cotton against the nail for a few seconds.

*

If your cat is too tough to handle, let your veterinarian take over the job. But if you train your cat early in life to let you handle its feet, you should be able to give it a manicure regularly without a lot of brouhaha. Holding the animal in your lap is the best position for both of you.

*

If, in spite of daily grooming, your cat develops "stud tail," the accumulation of oil just below the tailbone, which is both unsightly and aggravating, bathe the area in a mild detergent. The next step is to dust with a medicated powder (check with your veterinarian for a recommendation) which will absorb the oil without hurting the fur or skin.

*

Another gadget on the market which some cats—and their owners—enjoy is a special pet-grooming attachment for the vacuum.

*

The rewards of daily good grooming of your cat are better health, a lustrous coat, and a friskier disposition.

The Cat's Bath

Most of the time Tabby is shiny, fur-licking clean. The cat's got her tongue—and a sandpaper-stiff one, too—to keep up appearances.

*

There are certain occasions, however, when a bath is imperative. The occasions are these: Tabby has gotten herself thoroughly mixed up with grease or oil and can't be expected to clean herself without some help; Tabby has a bad case of fleas and could use a flea shampoo; Glamour Puss is entering a cat show.

*

If your cat needs a sudsing, bathe her with a friend's assistance. Another person on the brigade is of enormous help. Although all cats can swim, and some even like water, only the show cat is inclined to be docile in a bath—and even Glamour Puss would prefer being somewhere else.

*

If you don't have a friend to help you bathe Miss Puss, place a small washable rug or folded turkish towel over the side of the basin or tub. She will be able to cling steadfastly to the rug during the entire bath while you hold her with one hand and scrub quickly with the other.

*

Before the bath, assemble these supplies: a pet shampoo that doesn't sting the eyes, a washcloth, two thick, absorbent towels, cotton, white vinegar, comb, hair dryer (optional).

A double kitchen sink—one side for soaping, the other for rinsing—makes an ideal bathtub. So do two plastic dishpans, or the old-fashioned laundry tub which is deep enough to discourage Tabby from climbing up the sides. The bathroom sink is possible in an emergency, but it is really too shallow and small to be practical.

Since a cat gets colds easily, avoid chills by turning up the thermostat to 75 degrees or using an electric heater in the room.

If you don't want to get scratched, trim Tabby's nails ahead of time. (See "Grooming.")

Using warm (not hot) water, fill both tubs. While your friend gently immerses the cat up to its neck (being careful not to get its face or head wet), get ready to lather fast.

Your friend in need keeps a firm hold on Tabby while you lather. Don't use soap around her eyes, ears, nose, or mouth. Wipe off her face with a damp washcloth. Swab her outer ears with a piece of cotton soaked in water.

Talk to Tabby gently and reassuringly as you work your way from shoulders to tail, being extra careful to remove any traces of stud tail—that brown substance that so often affects tails of males and some females.

When she is all clean, your partner can pick up slippery Miss Tabby and dunk her gently into the clear, warm rinsing water while you refill your side of the sink. Add a little vinegar to the second rinse to prevent tangles.

After the bath is over, wrap Tabby in one of the warm towels and put her in your lap for a rubdown and comfort. If it doesn't frighten her, use your hair dryer. It's faster. If she objects, use both towels.

When she's almost dry, let Tabby finish the job herself with her tongue. Yours is not to reason why a wet tongue helps in the drying process, but it works.

*

The finishing touch in Tabby's beauty bath is a comb-out.

For a long-haired cat, a half bath (in the soiled south half) is occasionally in order. Hold onto the cat with your left arm around the middle and sit it down into the suds. Scrub, rinse, and dry.

To avoid sniffles, don't let your just-bathed cat out for several hours.

Fleas

Some cats seem to be naturally resistant to flea infestation, even though they spend time outdoors. Other cats—by far the majority, alas—play unwilling host to fleas all or part of every year, depending on climate.

Fleas belong to the order of Siphonaptera. A flea's body is flat, dark brown, and small, covered with spines and bristles. A flea has no wings, but it jumps like a track star. It can't turn its head. It can move in only one direction—forward—and can scoot through the fur of its host like lightning. Each foot of the flea has two claws for holding on, and the mouth is so constructed that it can not only bite but suck. Blood is its food.

There are many kinds of fleas; the most common are dog fleas, cat fleas, and human fleas. The divisions are purely academic, however, since the fleas, unaware of such distinctions, happily cross over from one warm body to the next, and hang around any part of the animal or person.

Fleas take up residence on cats of all kinds, but particularly on the long-haired ones. It has nothing to do with general cleanliness or social status. Fleas are simply more at home on cats than anywhere else, though they will transfer their affections to you if no animal is available.

The eggs of the flea do not stay on the animal but fall off to hide in dark crevices, corners, or rugs. The larvae are maggotlike and legless. They last from one to three weeks if undisturbed.

Next, the larva spins a cocoon in which the pupa is formed. It remains in the cocoon throughout the winter, coming out in the spring ready to develop to the next stage: the adult flea.

The life cycle of the flea can run as long as one year; to get rid of a flea one must break up this stubborn cycle.

The flea spends only about 10 percent of its time on Tabby. The rest of its time is idled away in carpets, dark corners, crevices, bedding, or outdoors in the dampish places of your garden. Here's where the female lays her eggs, as many as five hundred at a time, and the cycle begins.

If the weather is very hot and dry and there is no cat in the vicinity, fleas will live only a short time. But let the weather become damp and fleas will multiply rapidly.

With a cat for a host, fleas can live from six months to three years. That is a lot of misery for Tabby. The itchiest thing in a cat's world is fleas.

Besides making Tabby thoroughly miserable, the blood-sucking parasites can ruin her coat, spread tapeworm, heartworm, and carry disease. Tapeworm larvae have been known to hitchhike on fleas. Cats can even get dog tapeworm from biting fleas that have been living on dogs.

Fleas can also carry serious disease from one cat to another.

Adult fleas also lay their eggs right on the cat.

How To Tell If Your Cat Has Fleas

The first symptom is, obviously, scratching. If this persists, examine your cat carefully. Part the fur around the neck and ears. If you see black specks (flea excrement) or the flea itself, Tabby—and you—are in for trouble.

Remedies

Sprays There are several ways to tackle the problem. If the cat is over three months old it can be sprayed with a flea spray *recommended by your veterinarian.*

The best sprays are formulas containing pyrethrins. Pyrethrins get rid of fleas in a hurry, yet are nontoxic to warm-blooded animals. Furthermore, they leave no hazardous residue in the house.

Do not use a solution made only for dogs.

Place your cat on a newspaper. Apply the spray close to the skin and concentrate on the extremities (neck, ears, groin, and tail), where fleas are apt to congregate. Avoid the face.

If the cat objects to the hissing noise of the aerosol can, apply the solution by hand, being careful to rub it in well.

Gather up the newspaper with the fleas that have fallen off, and burn it.

Another method is to hold the cat up by the loose skin at the back of the neck or have someone else hold the cat aloft. From a distance of six to twelve inches from the cat, move the can rapidly in a zigzag motion over the entire body, especially behind the ears and under the tail, until the entire coat is damp.

Repeat once a week, to be safe, for as long as the fleas seem to be present.

Powders A flea powder is another alternative. Dust the cat lightly all over, rubbing powder into the skin. This method is less effective than spraying and presents some problems in that a lot of the powder is inevitably ingested by the cat in its washing-up routine.

Never use a preparation containing DDT. DDT can kill a cat.

Drugs Your cat may scratch so much it develops sores, infections, or hair loss, for which a veterinarian may prescribe corticosteroids or antiinflammatory drugs.

✳

If the cat is badly infected, it can be given a bath with a special flea shampoo which you may obtain from your veterinarian.

✳

There is also a pill on the market which can be given cats to prevent fleas, but it takes almost a month to build immunity. If the cat already has the problem, pills won't help.

Flea Collars The chief pesticidal ingredient in the most popular plastic flea collars on the market is one of the organic phosphates. Flea collars impregnated with these chemicals are sometimes tolerated well by cats. Owners should also know, however, that they can cause systemic disorders in addition to various kinds of local skin problems, ranging from mild dermatitis to wet open sores.

✳

At an animal hospital in Pasadena, California, feline patients have shown symptoms such as vomiting, diarrhea, and fever—all correlated with a history of wearing flea collars.

✳

If you do put a flea collar on your cat, make sure you first hang it out in the fresh air for about two days. Then keep a close watch on your cat for signs of illness such as lethargy, a wobbling gait, diarrhea, or nausea. Inspect the neck area under the collar often for skin irritation. *Do not apply the collar too snugly*.

✳

One veterinarian also advises removing a flea collar every other day: one day on, one day off. Still another doctor suggests removing the collar every two weeks and keeping it off for two or three days.

✳

Keeping the collar off at night is also a sensible idea, says A.A. Barry, D.V.M., of West Lynn, Massachusetts. It prevents continuous inhalation of the pesticide when the cat is asleep.

✳

Never combine a flea collar with flea powder or flea spray. The double dosage could be a double whammy—right into the grave.

✳

I have not heard of good results with flea medallions, and my veterinarian tells me the toxic effects can be even greater than with collars.

Vitamins Large daily doses of vitamin B_1 (Thiamin) are often helpful in preventing fleas. Thiamin makes skin excrete sulphur, which repels insects.

Sprinkle a half teaspoon of brewer's yeast on each serving of food. Even if it doesn't keep off the fleas (and it is not always successful), the cat will love it.

What About the House?

Controlling fleas on Tabby is only half the story. If there have been fleas on the cat, there are flea eggs in the house ready to hatch into beasties on the hunt for an animal or you.

While it is relatively easy to get fleas off a cat, it is almost impossible to keep them off as long as the cat can go outdoors, or as long as there are dark, dusty corners in the house.

Fleas love basements, garages, and the ground under the porch. Naphthalene flakes scattered in corners where fleas are suspected to lurk will kill the larvae, but don't scatter naphthalene where the cat may step in it.

A handful of naphthalene flakes in the vacuum cleaner bag will kill the fleas in the carpet, where they often love to hide.

If the infestation is really acute, the only way to clean up the house is by fumigation. This is not as difficult as it sounds. Your veterinarian can provide you with an inexpensive insecticide bomb.

Follow the instructions carefully (and be sure to get the cat out before setting off the bomb), and you will have no fleas or any other kind of creepy-crawlie.

One Last Word

Don't delay solving the flea problem. Fleas are very detrimental to the health of any cat, being intermediate hosts to tapeworms and heartworms. They can also carry serious infectious diseases from one cat to another.

Furthermore, your cat doesn't really like to scratch. Neither do you.

Home Care for the Ailing Cat

Unlike dogs, cats don't feign illnesses to get attention. In fact, they're more apt to bluster through minor indispositions. So when Tabby acts sick, you can be sure she really is.

If your cat is under par, take its temperature before calling the veterinarian. You'll need a rectal thermometer greased with Vaseline. Put the cat on a table, tuck its head under your left elbow and gently insert thermometer into the anus. Normal temperature for a cat is approximately 101.5 degrees Fahrenheit. Slight variations are not unusual, but a degree higher puts it on the sick list.

To take a cat's pulse, feel for the beat on the inner part of the hind leg. The normal heart rate varies from between 110 to 130 beats per minute. Kittens have faster pulses than adult cats.

Animal hospital or home for sick Tabby? Provided you, the nurse, know what you're doing and the vet agrees your cat is better off, it's home, nine lives out of ten.

Although there are situations involving severe illness when hospitalization is imperative, cats often do not thrive in even the best hospital. The ambience is not to their taste. The ill cat can fall into such a deep depression that it can actually lose its will to live. Your constant attention and soothing words at home in its familiar surroundings can make the difference between getting well or giving up.

If in-hospital surgical procedures *are* necessary for your cat, get her home as soon as possible.

To give Tabby a pill prescribed by the veterinarian: sit her on your lap, tilt her head toward the ceiling with your left hand, and open her mouth gently but firmly. With your right hand pop the butter-greased pill, tablet,

or capsule down her throat, poking it over the bump in the back of her tongue.

*

Don't fill up Tabby with your own medicines if she's under the weather. Consult your veterinarian. Remember, you're the nurse, not the doctor.

*

Don't try to disguise medicine in Tabby's food. She won't buy it.

*

Administer liquid medicine to your cat with a plastic (never glass) medicine dropper, squeezing *a little at a time* into the back of the throat. Easy does it. Give Tabby time to swallow. You don't want to get medicine into her windpipe and choke her.

*

If your ailing cat's on an eating and drinking strike, beware of dehydration, which can set in before you know what's happening. To test for dehydration, grasp its skin between your thumb and forefinger. If it doesn't spring back normally, call your veterinarian.

*

If your ailing Tabby has stopped eating for more than three days, call your vet or take her in for examination. It may be time to start forced feeding—and fast. Pureed baby food with meat every four hours will give her the nourishment she needs and prime the pump to get her own appetite going again.

*

Handy utensils for forced feeding are empty plastic hypodermic syringes (with the needle removed, of course) from the animal hospital or small plastic squeeze bottles.

*

With Tabby on your towel-draped lap, tilt her head back to a forty-five degree angle. Drip pureed baby food from the squeeze bottle into the back of her mouth, SLOWLY and a little bit at a time, so she won't choke. Give her time to swallow between slurps.

*

If you can't manage to hold onto Tabby, place her in a pillowcase or laundry bag with only her head free. This is handy for both feeding and pill-popping.

*

If your cat's too sick to give a lick about cleanliness, be sure to keep it brushed and rubbed down. If its nose and eyes are running, wipe often with a tissue.

*

To bring a cat's high fever down in a hurry, wrap it in a towel and spray with cool water or immerse in a tub of lukewarm-to-cool water, being careful not to dunk its head under.

*

An ethnic version of home care for a cat with pneumonia is provided by David Rubin, M.D. He brought his cat, Alex, home from the hospital under prognosis of early death, heated up a large kettle of chicken soup, and fed it to Alex, a spoonful at a time, whenever Alex could swallow. For two weeks Alex dined on chicken soup every hour, graduating to small bits of chicken and cottage cheese. Complete cure! Mazeltov!

*

As you play your role as cat nurse, remember that Tabby needs more than medicine to pull her through. RX: affectionate stroking, encouraging words—all the TLC you can give her.

Care for the Elderly Cat

Tabby is growing old. She sleeps longer hours in her favorite chair, dreaming, perhaps, of other, more joyous days.

*

Like senior citizens everywhere, cats live out their lives and continue to brighten ours with just a little special care and attention.

How Old Is Old?

Like everyone else, a cat is only as old as it feels—unless, of course, it's ill. For the sake of averages, though, it is pretty well agreed among cat fanciers that Tabby's getting old at ten, good and old at thirteen, and really old at fifteen.

*

The life-span of the poor alley cat has been estimated at but a few years, while its well-cared-for cousin often lives beyond fifteen.

*

When a cat reaches twenty it becomes newsworthy and usually rates a picture in the local paper with a little story alongside it, outlining its formula for longevity.

*

Recent headliners included Peppy of Pomona, California, and Susie of Seattle, Washington, who posed for photographers on their twentieth birth-

days. Mike got his name in the Kingston, New York, paper when he turned twenty-one, and Duffy, in Columbus, Ohio, hit the ripe old age of twenty-four.

English zoologist Alex Comfort reported a few years ago that a female cat beyond the White Cliffs of Dover was thirty-one years old and had given birth to kittens at twenty-six.

The oldest cat on record was a tabby named Puss, owned by a Mrs. T. Way of Devon, England, who reached its thirty-sixth birthday November 28, 1939, and died the next day (*1979 Guinness Book of World Records*)!

When Tabby's ten, she's roughly equivalent in age to a seventy-year-old human being. Each succeeding year equals four years of human age.

Chasing girl cats, incidentally, instead of sitting around the house playing with his catnip toys, can rob Felix of a few birthdays. Neutered male cats have a longer life expectancy.

How to Cope

Your cat will reveal its advancing years. Geriatric Tabby will sleep more and play less; eat less and shun company. She'll resemble most people who grow old.

The changes will be gradual, almost imperceptible, but the signs of aging will be there if you look closely.

Aging Tabby depends on you to be ready and aware of all the ways in which you can make life more comfortable for her.

About that old cat of yours, the main suggestion we can make is that you let Felix enjoy his old age. Don't expect him to romp the way he used to.

On the other hand, be wary if he seems unwilling to ever get up.

Old cats, even very old cats, have random moments when they yearn to chase a fly or scale the easy chair. They still have appetites and they still get hungry.

If your cat isn't interested in food at all and never wants to leave its warm corner, you'd better call the veterinarian. It may be sick.

In any case, now is the time to start taking your cat to the veterinarian's every six months for a checkup. No point in waiting for danger signals such as blood in the urine.

A thorough examination will bring to light such disorders as arthritis, neoplasms, heartworms, cataracts, even such simple but uncomfortable things as tartar build-up on the teeth. The doctor may even have to pull a tooth or two. Don't worry; Tabby will do very well with fewer teeth than she was born with.

At this semiannual visit your veterinarian can also give the necessary shots against common ailments. If Tabby isn't responding to your calls the way she used to, the vet will check her hearing. Question him about possible changes in her diet, too.

Arthritis and Aspirin

Old cats, like old people, sometimes suffer from arthritis. Treatment can reduce the discomfort but it cannot cure the disease. Sometimes cortisone is recommended; other times, heat; and often, aspirin.

A lot of controversy surrounds the use of aspirin in treating cats. It was once thought that aspirin was a strict no-no. Now we know that *in correct dosages* aspirin is effective as an analgesic. Correct dosage is one *baby* aspirin (75 mg) for each six pounds of body weight, no more than once every twelve hours, owing to the cat's slowness in metabolizing the drug. Do not administer to cats that are not eating normally or show symptoms of kidney disfunction. *Liquid* baby aspirin is preferred by some vets.

Do *not* dose your cat with aspirin or anything else without explicit instructions from your veterinarian.

Nutrition

A nutritional program for geriatric pets takes many forms. Old Tabby, for instance, may have become more finicky than usual, owing in large part to a decreased sense of smell. Owners of such cats are advised to divide the daily ration into three small meals rather than two large ones.

Taste stimulants such as tidbits of their favorite meat or some egg may pick up sluggish appetites and forestall weight loss.

Less beef and more chicken, lamb, and cottage cheese may also be emphasized. The latter are easier to digest. For the same reason, dry food should be decreased or eliminated entirely.

On the other hand, as my veterinarian said: "Never upset a cat that is doing well. It *hates* change."

Always provide plenty of fresh water for your older cat. (For all cats, for that matter, no matter what their age.)

If old Felix starts drinking an unusual amount of water, check with your veterinarian. It could be a symptom of the start of kidney failure.

Ask your veterinarian if your cat needs vitamin and mineral supplements.

Exercise

If your cat is one of those settin'-'n'-a-rockin' kind who never even wants to look out the window, it might be a good idea to lift it up and bring it into the living room and play with it once in a while.

Obesity may become a problem if your Tabby is not exercising as much as in earlier years. Fat cats with sagging middles are sad to see—examples of indiscriminate feeding, poor care, and too little play.

*

Don't neglect giving the cat toys to encourage it to move around a bit.

The best rejuvenator of all is a younger playmate. I have sometimes adopted a kitten to brighten up the life of a feline senior citizen, and the results have been nothing short of miraculous. Suddenly Creaky Grandpa is chasing Small One all over the house as though he had just shed a generation.

Grooming

Older cats appreciate regular brushing and/or combing more than ever. Cats are increasingly subject to hairballs as they get older.

Be especially aware of chilling them when you bathe them, and don't let them be annoyed by fleas or ticks.

TLC

Just like people, older cats sometimes become crotchety and cranky. To keep personality changes to a minimum, it is a good idea not to switch routines.

Don't suddenly put their beds or feeding bowls in unfamiliar places.

If they are suffering from failing eyesight or have gone blind, don't move all the furniture around.

Unless they are already accustomed to such a daily plan, don't leave them alone for long periods of time.

Don't leave them with strangers in a new boarding kennel.

*

Above all, don't take your aging cat for granted. Shower him with love but don't fuss over him—a nice distinction.

*

Just think how you would feel if the roles were reversed.

*

The same blanket, please. A soft tone of voice. Lots of petting. Open the door. Shut the door. A lap.

What You Can and Can't Catch From Your Cat

Zoonosis: a word derived from the Greek, meaning a disease communicable from animal to man under natural conditions.

We all know about rabies. It has been controlled so successfully in this country that only a handful of cases is reported each year. We will not dwell on this disease. Instead, let's take a look at some of these other stories and try to separate fact from fiction.

There are probably more diseases your cat can catch from you than vice versa.

To stay healthy in any household with any animal presupposes ordinary common sense regarding sanitation and personal hygiene.

If you let your child play with cat feces, for instance, you are running serious risks no matter how disease-free the animal is.

What You Can Catch

Ringworm: If you notice your cat scratching itself, examine for fleas or skin lesions. The former are pesky parasites that *can* transfer their affections to people; the latter may be ringworm, which is one of the most common ailments we can catch from our pets.

Ringworm is a fungous infection of the skin, and is often hard to get rid of.

Stray cats sometimes have it and should be examined carefully before being taken into the household.

If you do catch ringworm, take both Tabby and yourself to your respective doctors for immediate treatment. A drug called Griseofulvin has proved highly effective.

Cat-Scratch Fever: No one knows exactly what causes this, but it may well be a virus.

＊

Cats supposedly transmit the disease when they scratch you, but no one knows for sure.

＊

The cat itself shows no sign of illness. Nevertheless, a child so affected may experience swollen glands under the jaw or in the armpit or groin, a low fever, loss of appetite, and sometimes nausea or stomachache.

＊

An adult usually experiences nothing more than an ache-all-over feeling.

＊

Drugs help very little, if at all; the malaise almost always clears up by itself.

＊

A thorough cleansing of all bites and scratches from the cat can help prevent infection.

Toxoplasmosis: A few years ago the media were in a terrible flap about the dangers to cat owners of toxoplasmosis—a word most people had never heard of, though the disease had been known since the early 1900s.

＊

Because the cat is a natural host for this one-celled protozoan parasite called *Toxoplasma gondii,* cat owners were told, "Beware!" After the shouting died down, veterinarians and scientists were finally able to make themselves heard, and the facts, as spelled out by them, were not as alarming as the newspapers had made out.

＊

"Toxo" is a disease that affects many birds and mammals. If a cat eats anything contaminated by *T. gondii,* its intestinal tract acts as a kind of incubator where thousands of these organisms are reproduced and released in the feces in the egg form called oocysts.

＊

About 90 percent of the time, the cat so affected shows no symptoms of the disease even though it is a carrier. It can, however, transmit it to its kittens *in utero.*

＊

Diagnosis of the disease can be made through stool analysis, determination of antibody response to vaccines (titer levels in the blood), and clinical signs, if there are any.

＊

In the few cats that show symptoms, the clinical signs include fever, jaundice, pneumonia, and sometimes anemia. It is a disease often confused with others.

*

Treatment of severe cases involves the use of sulfa drugs and pyrimethanine and is often drawn out and not too successful.

*

Because the great majority of cats with Toxo show no symptoms, the hue and cry in the media against Toxo was primarily directed at its danger to human beings via the household cat.

*

This danger is real, if remote. Primarily it is important to pregnant women who can, if infected with Toxo, abort or give birth to a child with birth defects. If, therefore, you are a pregnant owner of a cat or are planning a pregnancy, it would be a good idea to take your cat to the vet to be tested for Toxo. If it is positive, get the cat out of the house and submit to tests yourself.

*

Other precautions for pregnant owners:

1. Don't let your cat outdoors to hunt.
2. Don't feed it raw meat.*
3. Use rubber gloves when cleaning out the litter pan. Clean it at least once a day, and dispose of the entire contents.
4. Better yet, have someone else in the family clean it.
5. Don't eat steak tartare or any other raw or undercooked meat.
6. Wear rubber gloves when preparing meat.
7. Avoid gardening or digging in any soil possibly contaminated by cat feces.
8. Keep children's sandboxes covered. Cats like to use them as litter pans.

*The controversy over raw versus cooked meat goes on. A lot of vets and breeders still endorse supplementary feedings of raw meat and can point to healthy cats to prove it. Others have bowed to the Toxo scare and substituted cooked meat. Take your choice. Personally, I prefer raw meat for cats, and have never had Toxo to contend with in any cat.

*

Raw meat is obviously not the only source of Toxo. Much about the disease is still a mystery. Vegetarians, for example, display Toxo titers as high as omnivores. How are *they* exposed?

*

Also, one of the worst Toxo areas in the world is India. Yet there are very few cats and meat eaters in India.

80

Worms: Another ailment transmitted to people (usually children) by animals is visceral *larva migrans* (caused by larvae of the common ascarid, or roundworm, found in dogs and cats). To be infected, the human being must ingest infective ascarid eggs contained in dog or cat feces or dirt that has been soiled by their excrement.

Deworming of pets when young is an important precaution. See your veterinarian.

Worms are less common in kittens than in puppies.

Cutaneous larva migrans (caused by larvae of several types of hookworm that infect dogs and cats) occurs chiefly in the southeastern part of the United States. The larvae get under the skin and cause severe itching.

The most common internal parasites affecting children, however, are pinworms, and they *cannot* be transmitted by cats or dogs.

Allergies: Some people are allergic to the dander in the hair of cats. Antihistamines may control symptoms (not unlike hay fever) for some, but the best treatment, unfortunately, is the removal of the pet.

What You Can't Catch

Cancer: A few years ago newspaper reports would have had us believe human beings could catch leukemia from cats.

Although cancer *is* a common disease of cats, there is no record of its being transmitted by them to people. If the disease were contagious, veterinarians, who handle such cases every week, would contract it. They do not.

It has been demonstrated that there is a 3 to 7 percent chance that a cat exposed to an FeLV-positive cat will become infected. In other words, horizontal transmission to other cats is possible; transmission to humans (except in a laboratory test tube) has *never* been documented.

Panleukopenia or feline infectious enteritis: This disease (sometimes called distemper) cannot be transmitted to people.

Respiratory diseases: Although there was one case of a person's contracting an eye infection identical to the virus causing feline pneumonitis, the incidence is very rare. More likely it's the other way around.

Haemobartonella: Feline infectious anemia, or haemobartonella, a form of anemia caused by a parasite in the bloodstream that eats the red blood cells, is not contagious to man.

*

You can get more illnesses from your spouse than from your pet, but if Tabby is sick, take her to a vet immediately.

*

Wash your hands after handling your pets. Keep the cat away from your food preparations. Change the litter daily, and keep outdoor sandboxes covered when not in use.

*

Don't neglect any animal bite.

CHAPTER THREE

Feeding for Good Health

Food Requirements of the Domestic Cat

Despite the prodigious amount of research on animal nutrition in the last twenty-five years, there is still less known about feline nutrition than about that of any other animal.

*

Most veterinarians will admit that there are few hard-and-fast rules about what to feed your cat, although experience and learning how to read the fine print on commercial cat food labels can set up certain guidelines.

*

The best indication of quality in cat food is the manufacturer's statement on the label that the food has been found to be adequate by the successful completion of the AAFCO (Association of American Feed Control Officials) protocol.

*

Another indication is often price. Cheap pet foods generally contain poor-quality protein and no supplementary vitamins and minerals.

*

The cat in the wild devours all its prey, including the entrails, which often contain digested carbohydrates. The domestic cat today is trying to adapt to our environment by eating man-made cat foods, but it doesn't always wholly succeed. Sometimes its teeth fall out at an early age; sometimes it gives birth to stunted kittens. All because of poor nutrition.

*

On the other hand, pet food companies have gone to great lengths and enormous expense to determine what a cat needs for optimum health. They cannot be faulted for sincerity or effort. Nor, in many cases, for their products, which often can be far better for cats than gourmet home cooking.

*

We do know that the basic requirements of the cat are protein (with high caloric density), fatty acids, minerals, and vitamins, all in correct proportions.

*

If you feed your cat a *quality* commercial cat food in both canned and dry forms, raw muscle and organ meat two or three times a week, and plenty of fresh water daily, you will probably have a healthy, well-nourished cat.

*

Water served in a glass or ceramic bowl (any material other than plastic) seems to taste better to cats. It should be changed every day, and in hot weather, twice a day.

*

(For reasons obviously not aesthetic, some felines prefer to drink their water from week-old flower arrangements, toilet bowls, and the pitcher you keep on the porch for watering the hanging plants. Unless you find this seriously offensive, relax. It won't hurt the cats. The only possible danger to them is in toilet bowls recently cleaned with a phenol-based product. It is my experience that cats don't like that water because it doesn't smell right, but don't take any chances—keep the lid down.)

*

The above is what a cat *needs*. What it wants is usually what it has been trained to eat from kittenhood—hence the importance of starting out with a good diet. A kitten weaned to a mono-diet will go on demanding its one food, refusing all others, and is going to display one or more symptoms of malnutrition.

*

Cats brought up intelligently like variety; and luckily, variety will go a long way toward guaranteeing a well-rounded diet. For instance, I buy six flavors of a meat-cereal combination canned food for my cats' breakfast and alternate them regularly so that the cats don't become hooked on any one flavor. Two level tablespoons mixed with a handful of dry food go into each dish. The dry food varies the texture and helps to keep tartar off their teeth.

For their evening meal, I may give them a quarter of a six-ounce can of meat (liver, kidney, chicken, fish, or combinations of these) fortified with minerals and vitamins according to the formula on the can, mixed with a handful of the dry food.

*

Or two or three times a week I give them a helping of raw beef cut in bite-size pieces, or one of the organ meats such as liver, heart, or kidney— beef or lamb, never pork. I am chary with liver—it is very high in vitamin A. Also very rich, and too much can cause diarrhea.

*

I give them tuna once a week. They would eat it oftener, but too much can cause inflammation of body fat, which is called steatitis.

*

Treats are permitted. A spoonful of cottage cheese or a small helping of yellow cheese are excellent sources of calcium.

*

Other table scraps cats love on occasion are roast lamb, deboned chicken, beef, bacon (just a little, please), and raw egg yolk. Never give them raw egg white, as it destroys the vitamin biotin. Cooked egg whites are fine.

*

Semimoist cat foods are palatable to some cats (though not to others) and are easy to serve. This makes them, along with dry food, especially convenient for traveling. However, they are relatively expensive and high in phosphorus. Better not offer semimoist foods except for occasional variety.

*

Never feed your cat an all-meat (high-phosphorus) diet. It will result in a gross deficiency of calcium, for one thing. Kittens on an all-meat diet develop weak, spindly bones.

*

Cats like and tolerate some cooked vegetables very well. These include carrots, beets, turnips, green beans, lima beans, corn, asparagus, mushrooms. These can be mixed with their regular canned food. Many cats also love, for reasons unknown, cantaloupe. I also had a cat once that went mad over artichokes. I taught him to hold the leaf between his front teeth while I pulled. One leaf for him; one leaf for me. We divided the heart. He didn't care for hollandaise.

*

A cat who has developed a taste for sweet corn often learns to eat it, balancing the ear between all four paws, lying on his back like a Roman and munching his way around.

Another cat that garnered a lot of publicity ate his ear of corn on a skewer slung between two posts that his mistress had built for him. In corn season, he ate two ears a day—with butter.

*

There is also evidence that some cats will go for raisins, cooked rice, and tomatoes. In Italy, a lady spilled some olive oil on a wad of lira. Her pet cat ate the whole bundle.

*

Some veterinarians advise adding a teaspoon of oil daily (cooking oil or butter), but I have never felt my cats needed this addition. Their coats are glossy without it. It won't hurt them, however, and some commercial foods do lack fat.

*

Mineral oil should not be fed to a cat, even for laxative purposes. It interferes with fat-soluble vitamins in the cat's food.

*

If your vet suggests vitamin and mineral supplementation, okay. Otherwise, skip it. You may do more harm than good. Oversupplementation with vitamins A and D is a common mistake.

*

I do add a quarter teaspoon of brewer's yeast to my cats' food on the theory that it helps to prevent fleas and because they love the taste. It also adds much-needed thiamine to the diet.

*

No milk is served my cats because they cannot digest it. If *your* cat can, fine, but don't serve it as a substitute for water.

*

How often should you feed your cat? Twice a day (breakfast and supper) is generally preferred, though many adult cats do well on one meal a day (morning) with only a small snack at bedtime. How much should you feed your cat? Use common sense. Be guided by the cat's appetite, how healthy it looks, and how it behaves. In short—not too much but not too little.

Kittens Need More

After weaning, kittens should be fed at least four or five small meals a day. Meaty baby foods or canned cat food can generally be used immediately, adding a little dry food (kitten formula) as the teeth develop.

Some milk may be given if the kitten can digest it. Watch for diarrhea. A kitten needs around 32 percent protein; a cat's needs are lower—21 to 25 percent.

Because a kitten's protein requirements are higher than those of a cat, I have usually added small balls of raw ground beef to a kitten's canned food, though an all-meat diet would be as bad as an all-carbohydrate one, resulting in an upset calcium-phosphorus ratio that could be fatal. Meat has little calcium and a lot of phosphorus. The ideal diet ratio is 2:1, or spindly bones result.

The frequency of meals should be decreased gradually as the kitten matures. At six months it is usually down to the two-a-day adult schedule.

Greens

If your cat is nibbling on your household plants—some cats do; others don't—never mind trying discipline. The cat is craftier than you are. The answer is to give him his own plants so he'll leave yours alone.

Take a shallow, fairly large soup dish, and fill it to about one inch from the top with good soil. Sprinkle on a good supply of oats, and add another layer of soil on top of the seeds. Place the dish in a sunny window, water well, and wait for the first sprouts. In a week they should be a couple of inches high. When they are about three inches tall, offer the dish to Puss and see if he will take his salad neat. Chances are good that he will plough right in.

Plant a new dish before the first one is down to the nub. You can vary the mixture with parsley and radishes. A little greenery every day is good for Puss, though no one is quite sure why.

What to Avoid

Cats require much more protein than do dogs. This is one reason, among several, why you should never feed a cat dog food. Cats have different dietary requirements.

*

Avoid food cold from the refrigerator. To prevent stomach upsets, always let it warm up to room temperature or heat it slightly before serving. It should not, however, be *hot*.

*

Do not serve raw fresh-water fish. It contains thiaminase, an enzyme that destroys some of the B vitamins.

*

Don't give your cat chicken, turkey, or anything else with sharp bones. They can splinter in the throat or pierce the gastrointestinal tract.

*

Stay clear of sweets of any kind. Cats can't taste sugar and it is as bad for them as it is for us.

*

If your cat has developed an exotic taste for hot dogs, pizza, beer, or tartar sauce (to name only a few), tell him to knock it off. All the above foods are bad for Puss.

*

A few cats have been brought up as vegetarians. It *can* be done, believe it or not, but it is definitely not advised. An exclusive diet of vegetables will lead to degeneration of the retina and eventually to blindness. Cats have to have the amino acid *taurine* in their diet. Fish and meat are high in taurine.

*

Don't serve all their dietary requirements at every meal. Use common sense by mixing one or two and covering the whole ground in a week, not a day.

*

A cat doesn't need a ten-course meal; it does need variety.

Fat Cats

If your cat becomes pudgy (and you can tell a fat feline just by looking at it), cut its food intake in half to induce weight loss. Once the optimum weight

88

is reached, feed enough to maintain the cat at this weight. Obesity shortens a cat's life span, and I have seen many fat cats in my day, which contradicts the general notion that they know enough to eat just what they need and no more.

*

The heaviest cat on record (according to the 1979 *Guinness Book of World Records*) was eight-year-old Tiger of Essex, England, who weighed in at forty-three pounds. His owner put him on a diet and he lost half a pound!

*

If your cat is fat, look at your waistline. Most fat pets are owned by overweight owners.

*

There is no ideal weight for a cat, any more than there is for a person. Body structure differs. There are males that look like halfbacks and males that resemble ectomorphic poets. Males always weigh more than females, unless you have the dowager type, who has gone to fat. My male cat weighs fourteen pounds and my female (his litter mate) weighs nine. Both are well nourished and neither over nor under their normal size.

*

If your overweight cat does not seem to lose weight by ordinary diet methods, you may want to look into one of the following prescription diets, so called because they are available only on prescription from a veterinarian. The foods on this diet are fine when necessary for the treatment or prevention of certain disease conditions such as kidney problems, heart conditions, bladder stones, and so on.

If Your Cat Won't Eat

Finicky is the word for feline. Felix, hungry as he is, takes one sniff of his breakfast, lifts his tail haughtily, and stalks away. Yet it's the exact menu he ate with pleasure the day before.

*

You know you've goofed as Felix's chef if he gives your offering the ultimate insult by scratching all around the dish, trying to bury it.

*

Your cat has another way of saying "Yu-c-c-ch" to its food—by dropping a piece in the water dish.

*

If your cat is turning up its nose at your menus, there could be reasons other than pure pique.

Cats are much more enthusiastic about food from a freshly opened can than from one that has been hanging around open in the refrigerator for a couple of days. Keep unused portions in a covered dish.

Felix doesn't like icy food, and it isn't good for him. All food should be served at room temperature.

In seasons other than summer, just leave the can out of the refrigerator for a few hours. In warm weather, keep it refrigerated and warm it slightly before serving. Serve water cool but not ice-cold.

Cats are worse creatures of habit than two-year-old children. Just try to palm off a can of supermarket bargain goodies or even a gourmet tidbit you bought as a treat, and watch the reception. Chances are ten to one your feline will turn up its nose.

If Felix is being stubborn about trying a new flavor, leave his dish out at least an hour to test his will power. Chances are, if he's hungry enough, he'll come back and dig in. Many cats, unlike dogs, are snackers.

If Felix refuses the new taste after it has been in his dish for an hour, throw away the food and let him go hungry until dinner. Then serve him something you know he likes. The next morning reintroduce the same new food he turned down before.

If after three days of trial your cat has not relented, don't buy the new food anymore. After all, some children never learn to like parsnips. Or next time, mix a little of the new food into the familiar old variety. Gradually replace old with new and you're home free. This works well with some cats, not all.

From the beginning, don't let your cat get used to a mono-diet of its favorite foods. And don't rely on Felix's taste buds to determine what is good for him. Maybe he's a tuna freak or a raw-liver lover. Either entree as an exclusive diet is neither healthy nor wise. Once a week is often enough.

You may be feeding your cat too often. Only kittens need to be fed three or four times a day, and a cat stops being a kitten after six months. From then on, a feeding night and morning is quite sufficient, and some adult cats do well on one meal a day.

If you are going by your own digestive clock and slipping Felix a little lunch, don't be surprised if he's downright picky at dinner.

If he continues not eating, the cat may really be sick. Anorexia (loss of appetite) is one of the first signs of illness in a cat. If Felix hasn't tasted any food for two days and seems depressed and lethargic, he's not being finicky, or playing games. He's sick. Get him to the vet fast.

CHAPTER FOUR

Kittens, Kittens, Kittens

Reproduction

A female cat usually comes in heat around six months of age, in the spring. Individuals may vary by as much as three months. Persians and Himalayans are inclined to be on the late side; Siamese are early. The period also varies, but generally lasts from four to ten days. On the third day the ovaries are ready for breeding.

Signs of estrus are comical and poignant: Miss Puss will rub your socks off, beg to be petted, rub her face on the floor, roll, and writhe. If you pat her, she will crouch down in front, lifting her rear end. Then she repeats the performance, adding to it that special cry that is not for you but for her One True Love. If she is not mated, things will quiet down after estrus for about three weeks, then start up all over again until fall.

It is known that light affects reproductive cycles in many animals, including cats. In the Northern Hemisphere, cats normally do not come into heat between early October and late January. A commercial cattery therefore has problems if it wants to produce kittens for Christmas. If a fluorescent lamp of 5000 kilowatts is installed in the queens' (as breeding females are called) room, however, and adjusted to fourteen hours on and ten hours off, the queens can be bred throughout the winter season.

Some female cats (especially those kept indoors) cycle all year long. This is more true of shorthairs than of longhairs.

Is Your Cat Expecting?

The time has come and gone when, for Mrs. Cat, life could be described, in the immortal words of Mehitabel, as "one damn kitten after another." Everyone, from the humane associations and departments of animal regulations to veterinarians and just plain folks, now urges the neutering and spaying of all cats unless they are purebreds.

Cats still become pregnant—by design and by accident. Classy cats are mated to perpetuate the best points of their breeds. For them, maternity care before, during, and after birth is as fussy as anything you'd find at the nearest lying-in hospital.

The expectant cat outside the classy cattery needs midwifery help too. If your Tabby becomes pregnant—either because you really want kittens and have homes for them, or because she came in heat before you had her spayed and found her true love sauntering by—there are some things you should know.

It is true that millions of kittens have been born without benefit of help from humans, but as one who has midwifed her share of kittens, I can tell you that a little savvy comes in handy.

Prenatal Care

The most important facet of prenatal care is diet. Unless your cat shows definite signs of illness—loss of appetite, depression, vomiting, diarrhea, inflammation of the breasts (mastitis)—your principal job during the sixty-three-odd days she is expecting is to see that she gets enough of the right food.

As with any mother-to-be, Tabby is going to be hungrier than usual. A light lunch of cottage cheese may be a good idea if she begs for food between breakfast and dinner. She needs all the calcium she can get.

A little egg yolk or hard cheese is also on the preferred list.

94

Extra fat and protein are a good idea at this time, and can be provided by feeding her snacks (small amounts only) of cut-up chicken or lamb, and by seeing that a teaspoon of vegetable oil is added to her daily menu.

Be sure lady-in-waiting Tabby has enough water. If she drinks milk (remember, not all cats do or should—it gives many of them diarrhea), offer it to her.

Don't let her get fat. The expectant cat is going to gain weight, obviously, but it is up to you to distinguish between the necessary extra poundage and sheer self-indulgence.

It is a good idea to take your pregnant cat to the veterinarian for a checkup about midway—say, in four weeks. The doctor can examine her, checking her nipples, gently palpating her abdomen, and sizing up her general condition, including weight.

Ask the veterinarian for some tips on kittening, what to expect, and what not to expect. You should know the scenario, even though most mama cats know more about giving birth than all of us put together.

*

Be sure to get the doctor's emergency phone number in case everything does not go according to plan.

Getting Ready for Kittens

When the witching hour approaches, queens will begin to hunt for a proper hideaway for the big event.

Long before that, you should procure a large box from the grocery store, with sides low enough for Mama to come and go easily but high enough so kittens can't climb out.

✳

Spread a thick layer of newspapers on the bottom of the box; cover with several layers of toweling.

✳

Don't put into the box anything so loose it might later smother a kitten.

✳

If Mama Cat has a favorite hiding place, such as the front closet, place the birthing box there and show it to her. Let her get used to it several weeks before the event. If she ignores it completely, you may be sure she won't use it when you want her to.

✳

When I was a little girl, my first cat, Kitty Puss, bulging with progeny, disappeared to parts unknown. We found her several hours later, at the bottom of a barrel in the basement, with five kittens, all happily sprawled on a set of broken dishes.

✳

A barrel is really commonplace compared to some of the other strange maternity wards that cats have been known to select. Would you believe an empty pot-belly stove? Or the space behind the seat of a firetruck? How about inside a Xerox machine?

✳

In Paterson, New Jersey, a mama cat with lofty ideas had her kittens in a tree and refused to come down for meals. Her doting owners conveyed rations up a ladder twice a day.

When Labor Begins: Progress and Problems

Don't leave town when Mama Cat is ready to deliver. Cats like to have their people with them when they are giving birth, especially if it's the first time. Your cat needs moral support for her Big Event, and sometimes she'll need more than that.

✳

Papa cats are also often welcome and can be of real help if they have sense enough to know what is going on. Even rejected suitors can help.

✳

A Siamese named Deuteronomy, belonging to a friend on Long Island, is a good example of what some male cats can and will do during labor.

96

Deuteronomy leaned his weight against his love all during labor, letting her push against him with each pain. He also licked her head frequently in what was obviously a comforting gesture.

When a new daddy cat is around after the birth, he'll sometimes babysit his kittens if Mama wanders off.

In most cases, there is nothing more anyone can do than to be there during the actual labor, offering reassurance, sympathy, and a watchful eye in the event anything untoward happens.

Birthing can take as long as twelve hours, but the average length of time is nearer to two.

Naturally, a large litter takes longer than a small one.

Each kitten comes in its own amniotic sac. Sometimes the sac ruptures before birth, staining the box with a pinkish fluid. Then sac and placenta are discharged later.

If the baby is still in its sac, the mother cat will break it, chew the navel cord, and eat the placenta, which follows. Be sure it does follow: a retained placenta can cause peritonitis. A good idea is to count: one, two, three, four—making sure there is one placenta for each kitten. Occasionally a cat doesn't seem to know how to break the sac, and you must do it for her or the kitten will quickly smother.

If the kitten doesn't breathe immediately, you can insert your little finger inside its mouth to clean out any material which may be impeding breathing.

Afterwards, gently pick up the baby with breathing problems by its hind legs and swing it ever so carefully, patting its back a little until it coughs and starts breathing on its own. Put the now-breathing kitten down for Mama to lick it clean and dry.

If the kitten comes feet first, it may become caught in the birth canal. You can help by VERY gently pulling on the feet with each contraction. But EASY DOES IT.

If the contractions continue for a long time without any kittens to show for it, call your vet immediately and report in. Your queen may need a Caesarian, and speed is of the utmost importance.

Afterwards

Your first job when birthing is complete is to make sure it really is. Carefully feel the mother cat's abdomen for a late-arriving fetus. It is not difficult to find. If there is one, don't wait too long for her to deliver it. It may be dead. Call your veterinarian immediately.

The next step is clean-up. Take out all the wet and dirty "linens" and replace them with clean ones. Turkish toweling is good because it can be easily washed.

For the next four weeks this box will be the sole home for Mama and her babies.

Although blind at birth, the kittens have already found their mother's teats and are kneading them with surprisingly strong little paws.

From now on, if all goes well, kitten care is Mama's job, while you look on with wonder and delight. She will nurse her babies, wash them, stimulate them to urinate and defecate, and clean up after them. The only times she will leave the box is to use her litter pan and to eat and drink.

Once her kittens are old enough to toddle outside the whelping box, she will pick each one up by the scruff of the neck and take it for its first venture into the big, wide world.

She will housebreak them (if her litter pan has high sides, buy a shallow one for the babies' use or build a ramp) and, with your help, encourage them to be weaned.

In four weeks, trim the kittens' sharp little nails, or else they'll injure a sibling.

If you don't want kittens running all over the house, confine them to one room. Or use a child's playpen with a cloth lining. It works like a charm. Mother can jump in and out but kittens are safe inside.

Now get your camera.

Orphan Kittens

Sometimes one is faced with the job of raising orphan kittens. One finds an abandoned litter or one's own mother cat dies before weaning her offspring. If you have the patience and stamina, you can do a pretty good job and the kittens will grow into healthy, affable cats. It is a big IF.

Don't rely on cow's milk; it doesn't have enough protein. Rush to the pet store or your veterinarian and demand a large supply of KMR, a commercial product whose initials stand for "Kitten Milk Replacement." It is a scientific formula ideal for baby cats that have no mama.

At the same time buy a Pet Nurser, a baby bottle designed for this purpose alone. Doll bottles don't work very well, and plastic medicine droppers, while permissible in a pinch, can allow milk to be aspirated if fed too fast.

The KMR formula should be fed according to the following ratio:

Wt. of Kitten	Amount of KMR Per day
3 oz.	1½ tablespoons
4 oz.	2½ tablespoons
6 oz.	3 tablespoons
8 oz.	4 tablespoons

The bathroom scale obviously will not do for checking the kittens' weight. Purchase the proper type (the kind with weights) and weigh the kittens every week.

This amount of KMR must be divided into five or six feedings per day. In the beginning, feed every three or three and a half hours; then lengthen the time to every four hours, then to every five hours. Start at 6:00 A.M. and make your last feeding just before you go to bed at 10:00 P.M. or 11:00 P.M. Kittens should then sleep through the night. Breeders who have raised dozens of litters swear by the above procedure.

Some vets advise feeding every two hours around the clock. This means you get little sleep and are good for nothing.

Warm the KMR to the same delicate wrist-testing temperature you would use on a baby.

The greatest danger in bringing up orphan kittens is to *over*feed them. Stick to the ratio noted above.

After the kitten has finished its meal, moisten a piece of cotton and gently massage its rear end until the kitten eliminates. This is what its mother would do if she were around.

Put each kitten back into the box. A large hatbox or the equivalent is about the right size. Across one end drape a heating pad turned to the lowest "on" position, and put a towel on top of the pad. (Don't overheat the room.) Kittens can crawl to the warm end if they are chilly or to the cooler end if they're too warm.

All healthy kittens sleep in a heap. Keep an eye on them. If they scatter, they are ill.

Weaning

Whether you are dealing with orphaned kittens or mothered ones, there comes a time—when the kittens are about four weeks old—when you will have to take a hand in the weaning process.

First, try to introduce the kitten to warmed milk in a dish (evaporated milk diluted with water, 50–50, is better than plain cow's milk) by dipping your finger in the milk, letting the kitten lick it off, then lowering your finger and his attention to the dish. It may take several tries before the kitten learns to lap. In the process it gets milk all over its face and frequently wades into the stuff. Eventually it gets the idea.

*

Some kittens do not care for milk at all (other than Mama's or KMR), and one should not force it.

*

Quickly supplement with baby foods—the meat and vegetable types. Most kittens love them.

*

I have always added raw ground beef rolled up in tiny balls, and hand-fed these morsels until the kitten learned how to eat them from the dish.

*

Gradually add small portions of canned cat food and, if the kitten will eat it, kitten-size dry food.

*

All foods fed to kittens (and cats), it must be repeated, should be served at room temperature or slightly warmer—never cold and never hot.

*

Kittens need four or five small feedings a day, gradually decreasing in frequency until by six months of age they are down to two meals a day.

*

Newly weaned kittens will continue to nurse intermittently for three or four more weeks, even if Mama tries to throw them out.

*

Fresh water must be on hand at all times. Milk is not a substitute for water. Watch for bad effects from cow's milk. Some cats have no problems; others do. If diarrhea occurs, remove milk from the diet.

*

By this time you have learned, we hope, how to pick up a kitten. Remember, it is not a sack of salt. One hand goes under its chest between its front legs, and the other, under its hindquarters.

Never lift a cat or kitten by its legs or stomach. Never lift a kitten by its neck—only Mama Cat can safely do this. Support a kitten or cat in your arms with both hands. Do not let the hind legs dangle. It gives any cat of any age an acute attack of insecurity.

By seven or eight weeks of age, kittens are old enough to be on their own and to be adopted.

Finding Homes for Kittens

Giving away kittens takes ingenuity, perseverance, a conscience about cats, and the imagination of a con man.

Kittens should be at least seven or eight weeks old before they're adopted. They should be eating solid food and be potty-trained. Above all, they must be *healthy*.

The first thing to remember is that a *bad* home is no solution to the problem.

Look around for a likely relative or friend first, especially if he or she is known to the animal, and amiable relations have already been established.

Avoid people who are away from home at a job all day. Kittens should not be left unsupervised, and need four meals a day at first.

If there are no friends or relatives available, try advertising in the local paper.

You can also post signs in supermarkets and on tree trunks and telephone poles in your neighborhood.

Don't take a box of kittens to the market and try to peddle them to passersby. It is an irresponsible way to find homes.

All applicants for kitten ownership must pass a test. They must be able to provide a proper environment, good diet, veterinary care (including inoculations and neutering at the proper age), and plenty of companionship and love.

A statement to this effect should be written out by you and signed by the person who adopts the kitten. Default means you take back the kitten and start over.

Once a kitten has been taken to its new home, you will have to follow up and see how the pledge has been observed. More than one visit is necessary. Ask to see proof of shots. At altering time, check to see if neutering was done. If the new owners have not treated their cat as well as they agreed to, take it back.

Hang tough.

False Pregnancy

False pregnancy is one of the more ludicrous conditions to afflict an otherwise genteel lady cat (or dog). Suddenly she begins to display symptoms of motherhood: her teats swell and become very pink, she looks a little baggy in the middle, and she may start acting maternal to a toy train or a set of blocks.

Reason? A sterile mating, say the authorities. My neighbors' cat is a good example. She came in heat shortly after they found her at the back door. Before they could get her to the vet, she mated with a passing tom. Then she was spayed. By that time ovulation had been induced and endometrial changes begun. The cat gave every sign of pregnancy for about a month, then the symptoms gradually subsided.

Cats rarely go to extremes during a false pregnancy (in contrast to some dogs), but occasionally a small dose of male hormone or tranquilizer is indicated. Let your vet decide.

How to Select a Kitten

We're talking here about a "cat cat"—a mixed-breed cat, formerly called an "alley cat" (a disparaging term never used by real cat lovers), or any cat that does not boast a pedigree. (For how to select a purebred, read the section, "If You Want a Really Classy Cat.")

"Cat cats" come in shorthair or longhair varieties, in all colors, and in several patterns (tabby-striped being the most common): calico, bicolor, tortoiseshell, and plain Heinz variety.

Some kittens find *you*. Many owners feel these are the best kind. Sometimes they are and sometimes not. Take your stray kitten to the vet for a complete overhaul. Ask him or her for advice. Watch the kitten closely for signs of illness. Kittens weaned too early need special diets, or they may have picked up mites, worms, or fleas—all of which will need attention.

Humane societies or animal shelters are often excellent sources for kittens.

Pet shops are generally not as reliable, though there are always exceptions.

If you look to neighbors or friends or ads in your newspaper offering "free kittens to good homes," make your choice carefully. There are important points to remember if your selection is to be intelligent rather than whimsical.

Health:

The kitten's *coat* should be shiny, clean, and without bare spots or sores. Its *ears* should be pink and clean; its *eyes,* clear and bright, without any signs of discharge. The *body* should be firm and lean, but more round than skinny. Feel the stomach: if it is distended, there is trouble. Around its *rear*, look for signs of diarrhea. The anus should be clean, without irritation.

Temperament:

Don't fall for the shy one that huddles in the corner. The best pet is the kitten who purrs when you touch it and who seeks you out. It should be friendly, playful, self-confident.

Be sure you can return the kitten if for some reason the adoption does not work out.

Take your new kitten to the vet for a checkup and inoculations.

CHAPTER FIVE

Behavior - Good and Bad

Some Feline Fables

No doubt about it, cats have had a bad press. Ever since *felis catus* wandered into town from the African desert to take up residence with man, legends and superstitions have been more popular than facts. Fallacies about cats range all the way from outright lies to half truths—and sometimes the latter are the most dangerous of all.

Cats Harm Babies

The most common myth about cats is that oldie: a cat will suck a baby's breath. How such a canard ever got started is a mystery. Perhaps a cat was glimpsed sniffing at the milk on an infant's chin and the child subsequently died of that sudden fatality, crib death. Whatever the source, this is a lie that dies hard. If you use ordinary precautions in introducing your cat to the newcomer and treat the cat with as much consideration as you would an older sibling, all will be well. It will want to inspect thoroughly, sniff a little, and perhaps give Junior a friendly lick. If the cat doesn't have fleas or other parasites and is in good health, it should be permitted to snuggle with the baby under your supervision. I grew up with a cat that always cuddled close to me at night—as have millions of other children—and was much the better for it.

Cats Can See in the Dark

While it is true that cats have beautiful and highly functional eyes with pupils that dilate widely to enable them to hunt at night, they cannot see in absolute darkness any more than you can.

In semidarkness, however, they do far better than man, which is one reason among many to keep your cat in at night unless you want him to kill baby birds that nest near the ground.

Cats Always Land on Their Feet

Here's a half truth often tested by small children fond of tossing Felix from the high-rise apartment to see what will happen. (See "High-Rise Syndrome.")

With more than five hundred voluntary muscles contributing to its unusual grace and suppleness, the cat does have a remarkable instinct to right itself in mid-air. There are, indeed, stories of cats falling from ten-story buildings and living to tell the tale.

The *whole* truth is that cats are frequently killed or maimed in short falls and do *not* always land on their feet.

Kittens, especially, can fall from heights as low as a couch and hurt themselves badly. Older cats have sprained hips or broken legs and necks falling from sinks, mantels, or enticing shelves.

Cats who live in apartments should be prevented from perching on balcony ledges or sitting in unscreened windows. It's a long way down.

Cats Never Overeat

Cats well-adjusted and happy in their homes generally do *not* overeat, though there are fat exceptions. Strays, however, who have known starvation and abandonment will frequently stuff themselves to the ruff over and over again in their anxiety that this meal may be their last, leading to nausea and diarrhea.

A Male Calico is Rare and Worth a Lot of Money

Male calicos—and/or tortoiseshells or any other three-color cats—are indeed rare. The female sex gene is linked to the color gene. However, when an occasional tri-colored male does appear, he is usually sterile, and even if he is not, he isn't worth more than any ordinary cat. Which is much or little, depending on how much you like him.

Cats Have No Moral Sense

If you mean "moral" in the sense of human society's codes and customs, you couldn't be more correct. A cat hasn't heard our rules about property or anything else. A cat lives by its own rules, and those aren't very far away from the jungle.

A good cat stalks and kills its prey, buries its excrement so it won't be followed, and steals any food in sight if it is hungry. That is the way to survive. Cunning is built into a cat's genes—and it's a lucky thing.

As for sex, the more, the better, say a cat's hormones. I once knew a man who gave away his female cat because she was so "immoral" as to go into heat before she had finished nursing her kittens and "did it" with a passing tom "right there in the driveway in front of all the neighbors!"

Moral: don't thaw the halibut when Felix is in the house, and spay or neuter your cats before puberty.

Cats Are Not Affectionate

It's true that cats differ enormously from dogs in how they express their love. Tabby won't wag her tail or make effusive noises like Fido. She'll give you the unmistakable message of her love, though, by rubbing against your legs, bumping her face against your hand, following you from room to room, and lying on your tummy if you're trying to take a nap.

As she kneads your body and purrs, you know she is saying: "I belong to this person."

Some cats are more demonstrative than others. My male cat cries to be petted. If I ignore him, he paces the floor until I drop everything and make up for his emotional deprivations.

The loudness of the purr has nothing to do with degree of affection. Some cats sound like motorboats; others play a more muted song.

Licking your skin is another sign of love pursued by many felines ignored by others. (Certain types of hand lotion, it must be admitted, also produce the same reaction.)

If you are sick, your cat will jump up to your bed and settle down to play Nurse Comfort all day. No better TLC in the world.

Cats don't like to be fussed over. Too much display of affection is embarrassing. Enough is enough. But try to deprive them of it altogether, and they can become traumatized into very skittery, neurotic cats.

Furthermore, cats have been known to grieve for dead owners, much the way dogs do. They will cry, stop eating, and pace the floor. Most such cats can be healed by being adopted by new owners who are sensitive to the cats' feelings.

The cliché that cats love places better than people can be put to rest too. A cat will move with its family with a minimum of fuss if a little consideration is given to its temporary sense of dislocation.

The stories of cats who have been separated from their families across hundreds, even thousands, of miles and who have found their way home across unknown territory, are some of the mysteries of science. If they didn't love their people, why would they try? (See "Cats and ESP.")

Some people want pets who are as dependent as small children. Others admire animals who treat you as their equal. Although there is something of the child in all pets and they need us for protection and love, those of us who are ailurophiles admire the self-sufficiency of the cat.

Whenever I look hard into a cat's eyes, he looks unflinchingly back into mine. What is he thinking? I wonder. And I never know. I like that too.

Cats Are Cowardly

This canard probably was coined by someone who watched a cat shinny up a tree just out of reach of a panting dog. Not all dogs chase cats, but enough do to intimidate most felines. If cornered, though, cats can usually hold their own.

Tales of how cats have played hero to their owners by alerting them to smoke in the dead of night, to poisonous snakes, or even to burglars climbing through the bedroom window, are legion.

Cats are just as courageous as dogs, though they don't make as much noise about it.

Cats Are Not Very Bright

Scientists have found that a cat's brain and our own do have things in common. We both have a brain stem that goes back to the reptilian phase of evolution, and a limbic system that governs bodily functions, instincts, and feelings.

In man the cortex has grown to huge proportions, and is divided into right and left hemispheres. The right brain handles emotions, intuition, and spatial awareness. The left brain controls logical deduction, language, and self-awareness.

Man is dominated by the left brain; cats are dominated by their limbic system and the right brain.

Perhaps this is why cats appear to have such psychic powers that they can turn on a heating pad just by willing it (see "Cats and ESP"), anticipate the ring of a telephone, know when their favorite person is coming home, and grieve when he dies, even if it is at a distance.

Probably no animal except the monkey is so skilled at getting in and out of confinement as the cat.

A cat's love of freedom may be partly responsible for this cunning. Many cat owners have learned to use this ability to their own advantage. Eric, a cat in New Hampshire that sleeps in the basement (warmer in winter, cooler in summer), lets himself into the living room at the head of the stairs by hanging onto the old-fashioned latch until it clicks, then pushing open the door. Saves a lot of scratching on the door.

Cats that go in and out of their houses and do not have cat doors have been easily trained to hit a cat-high bell to attract attention to their needs.

Other cats have even learned how to hang onto an ordinary door handle, give it a twist with their paws, and open sesame! No cure for this except a bolt.

Owners beware: when you take Tabby out in a carrier, be sure she can't pick the locks.

An open window protected only by a screen, can be dangerous to a feline who wants out. Even a tiny hole in the screen can be clawed to cat-size. When you leave the house, close the windows.

It is senseless to pit one animal against another. Dogs are expert at some things, cats at others, monkeys at still others.

The differences in learning ability among species are accounted for by the native dissimilarities in sensory and motor capacities, to say nothing of their inherited predispositions. Cats and dogs don't swing from trees.

According to animal behaviorist Benjamin L. Hart, D.V.M., Ph.D., writing in *Feline Practice* (Sept.–Oct. 1975), cats are capable of solving conceptual problems such as "oddity learning." In this type of experiment a cat must choose the odd article from three presented to it. For instance, offer the cat two balls and a square block. Choosing the block is the correct answer. When two blocks and one ball are presented, the cat must choose the ball to be rewarded.

*

Dr. Hart further asserts that in laboratory testing, cats and primates are the only species which can learn a task by observation. Cats that watch others learn such tricks as pulling on a string or pressing a lever to release a latch on a door learn much faster than cats who are learning from scratch. (Oops. Sorry about that.)

*

Cats have built-in clocks to tell them when to get up, what time dinner is served, and what day is Sunday (sleep late).

*

I have seen smart cats and dumb cats and loved them all. Not all cats are bright. Just like thee and me.

Male versus Female

I have noted that my female cats never wander farther than the next yard, and select outdoor sleeping places close to their own house. My males, on the other hand, no matter how home-loving and affectionate, have a wider territory to explore. Linus crosses the street and saunters up the sidewalk for a half block in either direction, calling on friends both feline and human. Lucy has never crossed the street in her life. Inasmuch as both cats are altered, it may be assumed the difference has something to do with gender and/or temperament.

*

In any household of several cats, there will be one Head Honcho to whom the others are submissive. H. H. asserts his dominance by cuffing his inferiors every once in a while, by lording it over them at meals (another good reason for always giving cats their own feeding bowls), and by occasionally keeping them off his favorite sleeping spots. When not busy making his point, H. H. lives without fuss with his companions, almost persuading them they are his equal.

Curiosity

Curiosity is synonymous with cat. Move a piece of furniture, take down a suitcase, open a cupboard door, and your cat will immediately come over to investigate. Curiosity in a cat has been explained by the fact it is by nature

111

a hunter. Whatever the reason, it can amuse itself for hours by exploring its universe.

Being naturally cautious, however, a too-dramatic change in environment may induce fearful reactions. This is especially true of loud noises such as a hair dryer or a vacuum cleaner.

Cats and Water

It is axiomatic, you say, that cats hate water. Let one get too near a garden sprinkler and it hightails it up a tree. This may go back to an instinctive knowledge, bred in the bone, that a wet cat emits more odor than a dry one, and in the jungle this could mean danger from enemies.

On the other hand, cats are nifty swimmers, and some seem to relish a little aquatic exercise now and then. One cat I knew regularly swam a few laps in the family swimming pool every day.

Other cats insist on bathing with their owners. One lady I knew had to be sure the bathroom door was tightly shut when she drew a bath or her Persian would jump in for a little paddle.

Another friend had a cat named Jason who insisted on showering with her every morning.

Faucets have long been known to fascinate cats. Many have learned how to turn on faucets—the kind one can lean against—and a dripping faucet is sometimes a cat's favorite source of drinking water.

If your cat is mad about water, the only things to be careful of are that it does not drown in a full tub when your back is turned (it has a hard time climbing up those slippery porcelain sides) or catch cold from splashing in the sink or under a faucet, as did one cat I knew. *He* ended up with pneumonia!

Play

Unlike a dog, a cat is one animal that doesn't need to be entertained. It is self-sufficient in its play to an extraordinary degree, but there are some things you can do to make the fun and games more interesting.

*

Playing is necessary if a cat is to preserve sleek muscle tone and keep its disposition alert and perky.

*

It is a cat's hunting instincts that direct most of its playtime activities. If you prefer that the mouse Tabby bags be catnip, see to it that it is. Some cats ignore catnip in any form, but the mouse shape and size appeal to all felines.

*

A string or piece of yarn becomes a slithering snake to stalk. Dangle one above Tabby's head and watch her jump and box. She may toss it up in the air and pounce on it. But better not leave her alone with it or you may spend the next hour pulling it, inch by inch, out of her throat.

*

Empty spools or hard rubber or plastic balls (Ping-Pong balls are the best of all) make wonderful prey for a cat's pouncing paw.

*

Avoid sharp or painted toys, however, or objects small enough to swallow, such as a marble or shiny button.

*

Rubber bands are favorites with some cats. They bat them around for a while and then chew through them like lizards' tails. Okay so far, but don't let them "eat the whole thing." Not good for the gizzard.

*

Spring toys that can be attached to scratching posts are favorites with cats, especially if they look like birds. (See "The Cat as Hunter.")

*

Paper has a fascination for many cats. I've known those that spend hours pulling Kleenex out of boxes or unwinding yards of toilet paper.

The empty brown paper bag is the best toy of all. Two cats and one bag equal a floor show.

*

Arthur, a British cat, longed to hula-hoop with the children in his neighborhood. His owner had a cat-sized hoop made for him, and Arthur became the neighborhood champion. Kept his weight down, too.

*

One of Felix's favorite toys—if you want to spend a little money—is a cat house. (I know, but what else can you call it?) Morris on TV calls his a good example of urban blight, but most cats adore them, appealing, as they do, to a cat's natural love for enclosed spaces. A good cat house is made of heavy paper or cardboard, designed with rooms on several levels, with doors and windows made for keeping an eye out for trouble. Felix or Tabby can spend hours going in and out or sleeping in the "patio." And it keeps them off *your* furniture.

*

The best plaything of all for a cat is another cat. A kitten will give pizzaz to Tabby, no matter what her age.

Cats and Other Animals

Who said the cat hates the canary? Some people are not aware that *Felis catus*, although a predator, has been known to make friends with almost every other animal in the kingdom.

*

If you already have one kind of pet and would like to adopt a cat, take heart. The combination, however unlikely, is not necessarily deadly. Which is not to say that precautions should not be taken—especially at first.

*

Unlikely companions of Puss can be divided into two general classes:
(1) animals whom Puss could attack and eat if he wanted to;
(2) animals who could attack and destroy *him* if they wanted to.

*

In the first group belong small delectables such as mice, rats, and birds. My files are bulging with photographs and stories of cats playing with white rats and mice and sharing their feeding dishes with mockingbirds and parakeets. This is obviously more easily accomplished when the cat is a kitten and more curious than fearful.

114

Adult cats, however, have also made friends with "prey." Two of my own once sought out and romped every day with a bantam rooster and a Belgian hare, both belonging to a neighbor. No one was ever hurt or even frightened.

*

The mothering instinct also plays an important part in cementing inter-species relationships. Mother cats have found and brought back for nursing baby possums, skunks, and rabbits, to say nothing of puppies.

*

Some cats even go in for rescuing stray baby birds that have fallen from their nests.

*

Other cats—of both sexes—have been known to lie down in hatcheries of baby chicks, apparently wanting to help nature along.

*

In the second category, larger "enemy" animals, the most common is the dog. Everyone knows of dozens of examples of lifelong dog-and-cat harmony, mutual protectiveness, and devotion. (See the section, "Why Not a Second Pet?")

*

Farm cats have also been known to adopt as constant companions other farm animals such as cows, horses, goats, and pigs. Never underestimate the adaptability of a cat. I even know of one that adopted a duck.

Cats and Music

Inasmuch as the hearing range of dogs and cats is much wider than that of humans (see "Ears"), it is not surprising that they are sensitive to music. German scientists at the Berlin Physiological Laboratory in the early forties studied a group of animals and decided both dogs and cats can distinguish between two notes separated by as little as one-fourth the range between two notes on the piano.

*

Though they can distinguish quarter and half tones, they seem to prefer harmony. If you want to find out the extent of your cat's musical appreciation, turn on the record player and experiment. Chances are your cat will tell you its prejudices by either hunkering down to enjoy the selection, howling in displeasure, or walking out of the room.

*

My own cats only display aesthetic pain over dissonance, atonality, coloratura sopranos, and unaccompanied violins.

They ignore a good deal of music, but listen with apparent pleasure to Mozart, Schubert, and Bach, especially if it is chamber music.

Your cat may prefer ragtime, band music, the harp, or Tschaikovsky.

Speaking of whom, a Siamese named Tybalt had a passion for the "1812 Overture." When the cat became lost on a cross-country trip, the only thing that coaxed him out from the brush after seventeen days of self-imposed exile was a version of the famous overture whistled badly by a desperate humane officer.

Cat Training

When Mr. Cat wants to know what to do in any situation, he asks himself, not you. The only time he will perform for you is when it suits his own needs or pleasure.

To teach such an individualist to live in the same world with us means we must go *with* the creature's grain, use extraordinary patience, not punishment, and compromise when necessary. Every cat owner draws a different line between essential discipline and indulgence.

Luckily for us, the cat is a tidy soul. Except for sick or disturbed cats, housebreaking is easier than with any other animal.

Mother cats train their kittens to use a litter pan. All *you* have to do is provide one, show your kitten or cat where it is, and keep it clean.

Not all cats seem to know their names, though they will usually respond to an imperative tone of voice they recognize as reserved for them.

If you reward Mr. Cat with a bit of food or petting when he comes when you call, he'll get the message, and show up ninety percent of the time.

Sometimes you can shriek yourself hoarse or rattle the dry cat-food box until your wrist hurts. Mr. Cat, though within earshot, prefers to ignore you. That kind of indifference is pure catness. If you can't take it, get a Poodle.

*

Naturally nocturnal, cats would much rather prowl than sleep at night, preferably outdoors, where they can hunt.

*

To train a cat to stay indoors at night and to sleep instead of play, sometimes takes a bit of doing, and once in a while it doesn't work at all. If your cat has totally refused to sleep indoors, if night after night he scratches on the door, ruining the panel, his claws, and your sleep, maybe you'll have to resort to more imaginative measures.

*

Some garages can be made safe and cozy for a cat, but many more are cold, damp, and full of their own hazards. It is possible, if you know a carpenter or a do-it-yourselfer, to build a little house for your cat in the backyard which he can use to come in out of the rain. I had such a house made for my cat, split-level, with wall-to-wall carpeting, and screened with heavy chicken wire. A heavy canvas flap kept out wind and weather.

*

Every cat must learn early in life what "NO! NO!" means. If you use those magic words in a loud, sergeant-major tone of voice, Felix will understand the second time he hears them.

*

Constant surveillance is also essential in training a cat to stay off kitchen counters or to keep its claws off the furniture. Unless you catch it in the act of misbehavior, your "NO! NO!" is wasted breath.

*

If you don't want Felix on your chairs, it sometimes helps to assign him one spot that is his. Cover it with a towel or small blanket and he will generally leave the rest of the furniture to you.

*

Scratching is doing what comes naturally to a cat. Ripping your newly upholstered couch not only gives Felix exercise but also removes his irritating nail sheaths.

*

Besides on-the-spot discipline, you can protect your furniture by clipping your cat's nails short at least once a month, if not twice. Another deterrent to furniture mayhem is a scratching post, preferably more than one. Putting one at the corner of the sofa or chair your cat has been mistreating will often do the trick.

*

Some cats *never* learn respect for furniture. Exile the cats from the upholstered areas and hope for the best.

*

It takes a bit of doing to train a cat to walk on a leash. If it's a Burmese or Siamese, it will take to the leash more readily than other breeds. Some mixed breeds also can be trained to a leash, though restraint is not natural to any feline.

*

Felix's leash training begins indoors. Put on a light-weight collar, loose enough to be comfortable but not so loose that it will slip over the head. Let him get used to this, then attach the leash and let him drag it around the house for a few periods of time each day.

*

While Felix is getting used to the leash indoors, make sure he doesn't get tangled in anything and become frightened or injured. After a few days' solo on the leash, pick up the end and follow him.

*

Don't try to lead the leash beginner. Let the cat go wherever it wants, but occasionally give the leash a little tug and direction. Make the walks short.

*

If an ordinary leash doesn't work, a figure-eight harness is sometimes more comfortable for a cat, and leading is easier. Don't use a dog harness—it is too stiff.

*

In a few days you'll know the truth: either Felix will walk on a leash or, not being a follow-the-leader type, he won't.

*

Another verbalization necessary in training a cat is a phrase such as: "It's all right." Easily startled, cats are sensitive, highly strung animals. The quiet voice in which you say these words will comfort the most skittery, especially if accompanied by stroking.

*

If you want to turn Felix into a stunt cat (a role he isn't comfortable with), work with him when he is in the mood to come to you for play and petting.

Look for some action he does naturally that is out of the ordinary and fun. Then try to get him to do it several times more, while repeating a command. Many cats turn out to be retrievers. If your pet shows any interest in running after a dropped object, it can be taught to bring it back by gentle encouragement and rewards.

When he performs, reward him with a bit of food he likes and plenty of flattery. Be careful not to tire the cat; its attention span is short.

How to Keep Cats from Scratching the Furniture

If you don't want your cat to fulfill its needs on your best damask couch, the corner of your velvet armchair, or your Oriental rug, you will have to go in for some fine and fancy training.

You will have an easier time of it if you can begin this training from the first time your kitten toddles out of the litter box. Every time Small One starts to shred the upholstery, say "No! No!" in a commanding tone of voice.

If Small One goes back to scratching the minute your back is turned, repeat "No! No!" and add to it the sound of a folded-up newspaper smacked across your hand. Cats hate loud noises.

Do not strike a cat. It accomplishes nothing in terms of controlling behavior, but it does associate your hand with punishment instead of petting. The cat that cringes when a hand approaches it is the cat that has been spanked. It's demoralizing for both cat and owner.

Because a cat must scratch something, provide it with a good scratching post. The post must be tall enough so the cat can stretch its full length to reach the top. No problem if we are still talking about a kitten. All you have to do is take its front paws, place them on the post, and go through the scratching motion. The Right Kind of Kitten will get the message loud and clear and forever stay off the furniture.

Unfortunately, many kittens and cats don't see it that way, and no matter how many fancy scratching posts you buy from the pet store or make yourself, they stubbornly refuse to have anything to do with them.

Certain kinds of materials are preferred over others, it seems. When I covered a post with leftover pieces of my nylon carpet, the cats loathed it. Ditto for shag. They like material that is woven in a linear direction—the same direction in which they drag their claws down. If you aren't sure which fabric is going to tempt Puss, look at what he has already ruined.

Or better yet, buy one from the pet store. Because the manufacturer has done his research, such a post usually fills the bill—for the cat that appreciates a post, that is.

To coax the recalcitrant cat, you can try putting some catnip under the top of the post or tying a spring toy to it.

Or change from fabric to cork or bark.

Some owners have found that to place the post next to the piece of furniture the cat has been scratching, will divert its attention to the right object.

One of those upholstered cat "trees" with numerous ledges for perching is also a deterrent to furniture scratching.

Covering the doorjamb with cork or the kind of carpeting cats like to scratch (tightly woven, not shag) will provide a dandy scratching area.

Tying a small bag of mothballs behind the scratched spot on the piece of furniture will sometimes discourage a cat. A few owners object to this method on the grounds that mothballs are poisonous to a cat. It is my experience that no cat would get within poisoning distance of a mothball because of the strong and objectionable odor.

*

If all else fails, a water pistol or plastic spray bottle filled with water is often very effective. It only wounds the cat's feelings.

*

There are products on the market that allegedly repel cats from forbidden areas. I hope they work for some people. My own cats thought they were Chat-nel No. 5.

*

Real problem cats who refuse posts and other diversions, to say nothing of ignoring your best training techniques, may have to be kept in areas of the house where upholstery is absent or at a minimum, and let outdoors to scratch.

*

If your cat is an indoor cat and has become incurably destructive, the last resort may be de-clawing.

*

No subject evokes more vehement protest from cat owners than that of de-clawing. Even among veterinarians there is controversy. Personally, I have never had a cat de-clawed, but I do not hold with some cat lovers that it is cruel and unusual punishment and should never be permitted under any circumstances whatever.

*

Removing the *front* claws only can be accomplished without trauma to the cat and with relatively little postoperative pain, provided the operation is carefully and skillfully done. I have known many cats that have had their front claws removed, and they live normal lives. According to the head of The Cat Clinic in my city, cats can defend themselves with their hind feet as well as their front feet. Sometimes better.

*

On the other hand, I would exhaust all other forms of retraining before I went to such extreme measures. But as an alternative to euthanasia, de-clawing is certainly to be preferred. Ask any cat.

How to Get a Cat Out of a Tree

There are two schools of thought on how to solve this problem: one advises calling in help; the other says to do nothing—the cat went up; the cat can come down. Personally, I have used both methods.

Firemen are quite familiar with cats in trees, as are telephone and power-company linemen and tree surgeons. It all depends on your own city which of these, if any, is likely to come to the rescue of your Tabby if she is up a tree and telling you in no uncertain terms she is too scared to make the return trip.

Tabby climbs trees because (1) they're there, (2) she enjoys the exercise, (3) she was getting away from a predatory dog, or (4) she was chasing a bird when, would you believe it, the birdie flew away and she was suddenly out on this skinny little limb thirty feet above the ground. . . !

The piteous cries from stranded cats, high in the windy world of leaf and sky, are enough to melt the hardest heart. Owner panics and calls for help. Whenever I have done the same, everyone is busy, including the Animal Regulation Department. Once my cat stayed up for three days, and was finally brought down by a tree topper. Tree toppers are good people to remember in this kind of crisis.

Another time, I was able to coax my cat down by making chirrupy sounds of encouragement. It took forty-three minutes but it was worth it.

The reason a cat is brave on the way up and terrified on the way down is because his retractable claws are so designed that when unsheathed, they quite easily clutch a surface, but only going up. When headed south, the cat must slip and slide, stopping every few inches to dig in its claws. A scary business.

Or, of course, the cat could back down. In all my years of living with cats, I have never seen a cat go into reverse gear, though one of my correspondents claims she has a cat that always descends in this manner. Smart cat.

If Tabby is up a telephone or power pole, the danger is even greater for cat and rescuer alike, considering the propinquity of high-voltage lines.

If your cat is up in the air, only you can decide whether to enlist help or wait it out. If you choose the latter, food is sometimes an inducement to descent, and you can try rattling the dry food box.

Spraying water from above—another favorite remedy mentioned in the books—is often quite impossible, but has been known to work if you can get up that high.

Whatever you do, don't try to play Tarzan yourself and climb the tree. Chances are you'll get stuck too, and then there will be two creatures to rescue—unless, of course, Tabby has scampered past you to land on the ground with a thump and a smirk.

Catnip Craziness

Catnip, or catmint, as it is called in England, is a hardy perennial herb native to the Orient and Europe, but now spread around the temperate areas of the world.

Lions lust after catnip; bobcats, leopards, jaguars, and lynx can be lured by its intoxicating aroma. House cats go bananas over it. And nobody knows exactly why.

The ordinary mint one grows for juleps and iced tea certainly doesn't turn felines on, but just rub a few leaves of catnip between your fingers to release the volatile oil, and presto! Felix goes wild.

Only very young kittens and an occasional adult cat fail to respond to the tantalizing smell.

Once I experimented with my Linus and Lucy, who had been exposed to numerous catnip mice too lightly impregnated with the fascinating odor to do more than inspire a fainthearted toss, but who had never met the pure stuff.

I put a teaspoon of the crumbled herb into a large brown paper bag, put the bag on the bare floor, and invited the cats to inspect it. In they went, heads first, rear ends twitching. They seemed paralyzed for about ten seconds, and then all hell broke loose. The cats swiped at each other. The fur flew. What was this? Catnip is supposed to induce glassy-eyed euphoria. It is a trip, not a tantrum.

Thinking Lucy wanted the bag for herself, I put down another one for Linus and he disappeared immediately into the paper cave. Silence. Both cats crawled out, dusted with catnip, and began to twist themselves into serpentine contortions. They rolled over, rubbed their faces on the floor, and purred like twin motorboats. About ten minutes later both cats walked off, apparently having had enough of this foolishness. In an hour Lucy strolled back into the room, walked over to the place where the catnip had been, and rolled over again with a sappy look on her face. If I hadn't known it was impossible, I would have said she was in heat.

This resemblance to estrus has led some scientists to infer that catnip has aphrodisiac powers. Not so, say others.

G. F. Palen and G. V. Goddard experimented with catnip and male and female cats, both altered and unaltered. About half of each group responded to catnip; age and sex were no factor. The experimenters concluded that though the behavior is very similar to that of estrus, the gonads are not involved (see *Animal Behaviour* 14:372–377, 1966).

Perhaps catnip has something to do with altering skin sensitivity. This might explain the face rubbing and the rolling, but certainly not the other expressions of rapture such as jumping straight up in the air or flying across the coffee table.

Catnip does not seem to have harmful effects of any kind or to be addictive.

No cat I ever knew expressed any particular desire for catnip unless offered some, or withdrawal symptoms if denied it. Nor do the effects appear to last longer than fifteen minutes or so.

It is fair to say that while catnip is not a narcotic in the usual sense, it is certainly a tonic, acting in some unknown way on the parasympathetic nervous system.

If the odor is too strong, some cats will walk away from it, and about one in ten thousand displays allergic symptoms to it.

To most cats it is a mysterious turn-on, a mood elevator, a good if non-habit-forming drug, the effect of which, like alcohol on humans, is at first a stimulant, then a tranquilizer.

The calming effect of catnip has long been recognized by breeders, who often use it in shows to keep Lady Tabby quiet during the long hours of judging.

If you want good quality catnip for your cat, grow it yourself. Seeds and plants are available at most nurseries. If you opt for the former, start it indoors in a pot (one with a hole for drainage, and use good potting soil) in a spot that gets good light but no direct sun. Keep it moist. When the first shoots appear, move the pot into the sun.

When the plants are about two inches high, thin them out and plant in other pots or transplant them into your garden, about six inches apart.

If you plant seeds directly outdoors, do it no earlier than spring, and sow the seeds fairly close together, following the directions on the package.

To avoid having plants thrashed by wandering felines, protect them with chicken wire or something equally tough.

*

As soon as the flowers are in bud, the leaves can be cut for drying. Hang small bunches of the herb in a warm place, such as a corner of your kitchen, and in a couple of weeks you will have enough catnip for a pride of pusses.

You can also try a little fresh catnip on your cat. Some cats like it better than the dry. But rub it between your fingers first to release the fragrant oil or Felix won't give it a second sniff.

If you wish, you can make toys. Instead of a mouse, just stuff little balls made out of a cotton fabric.

Although catnip is supposed to be strictly for cats, it wasn't always so. In the not-too-distant past it was brewed for an aching tooth or infant colic or just to vary the flavor a little in the afternoon teacup.

Brew yourself a pot of catnip tea someday and share a smirk with your favorite feline. But keep your feet on the ground.

Cats and Collars

Ask any cat and he will tell you that collars are for dogs. In this complicated, citified world cats can get used to restraint and all the impedimenta that go with it. In fact, there are many times when a collar is a good idea.

No cat takes to a collar with overflowing enthusiasm—at least, not at first—especially a long-haired cat. It may spoil his handsome fur.

What Kind of Collar?

The best kind is leather with an elastic insert. Plastic is less satisfactory—it's harder on the fur and less "givey."

*

The collar should be light in weight, but not so narrow that it cuts into the flesh.

*

The elastic section lets the cat pull out of it in case of emergency.

*

Be sure to choose a collar that is recommended for cats, not dogs.

Fit?

The collar should fit snugly but not tightly. You should be able to get two fingers inside the collar.

*

Check the fit often. Kittens grow fast. There is nothing more pathetic than a fully grown cat with a neck that's tiny from wearing a too-tight collar when young.

Attachments

If you are going to put a collar on your cat, you might as well make it serve a purpose. Attach a tag with your name, address, and phone number inscribed. It will help strangers to return him if he strays.

*

Some people attach a bell to the collar in the fond hopes that it will discourage Felix from killing birds. Personally, I have never known an intelligent cat not to figure out a way of stalking prey without ringing the bell. However, it may give you a sense of virtue.

Housebreaking Problems

Like his feral ancestors before him, Felix, the outdoor cat, instinctively digs a hole, urinates or defecates, then covers the evidence so his enemies won't find him.

*

The litter pan is an imitation of the outdoors, brought indoors to convince Mr. Felix it is okay to dig here as well as there.

*

Litter-ally speaking, you don't have to invest in an expensive pan for your kitten. A plastic baby bathtub or a plastic dishpan will do just fine for most cats. It must be big enough so an adult cat (kittens become cats in six months) can comfortably sit down in it.

*

Stick to metal or plastic for the litter pan. Wood and cardboard retain odors, and cats are ultra-fastidious.

*

Some cats become so dependent on their litter pans that with the whole backyard at their disposal, they'll demand to be let in if they have that urge. (Better this idiosyncrasy than others!)

If the kitten goes straight to the litter pan the first day it moves in, you can thank its mother. If Mama Cat herself was trained to the pan, she'll teach her babies to use one by the time they can toddle into it.

*

If your kitten was adopted too soon or was picked up as a stray with an unknown upbringing, it may balk at the litter pan. Put it into the pan, then take its two front paws and gently go through the scratching act.

*

If your kitten can't climb easily into the litter pan, provide a ramp. It will learn the way immediately.

*

Even for this ultra-clean animal, housebreaking problems do sometimes arise. Don't panic if your cat refuses to use the litter pan. It undoubtedly has a good reason—good from the cat's point of view, that is. All you have to do is to figure out what it is.

*

Your cat will take its business elsewhere if you don't keep the litter pan impeccably clean.

*

Empty the litter pan at least once a day, wash it with soap and water, and refill it with clean litter. (I clean my cats' pan every time it is soiled with a bowel movement. If I don't, they tell me about it.)

*

If you use a disinfectant or cleanser on a litter pan, be sure to rinse thoroughly. Felix turns up his nose at chemical odors, too.

*

One litter pan and more than one cat, or one litter pan and a big house could spell trouble. Provide several, if needed—one upstairs and one downstairs in a two-story house. Or one at the back door and one at the front. Kittens are especially prone to being caught short, and shouldn't have to trot too many yards to the latrine.

*

Don't keep moving the litter pans around to suit your latest décor. Cats like their bathrooms to stay put.

*

Cats also don't like their litter pan too close to their eating area. Would you?

If fastidious Felix suddenly starts using the living room rug as well as his litter pan and is squatting all over the house, crying frequently, beware. He may have early stages of cystitis, a common urinary problem of cats, especially males. Call the vet. (See "Urinary Problems.")

Sometimes your housebroken cat gets so upset by a new baby or pet or change in a household routine, it will vent its frustration on your bedspread, brand-new carpet, or some other forbidden territory.

If Felix has developed socially unacceptable bathroom habits, try putting him in a small room (or outsized cage) as bare of furniture as possible, except for the litter pan. The choice will be his: use the pan or soil his own nest. Applaud the right decision.

The most annoying problem is spraying. A male cat will usually start spraying at about nine or ten months. This is instinctive territorial marking. To avoid this nuisance, have him neutered at seven months (or eight months if he has not matured enough) before he has learned how. Females sometimes spray, too, though this is less common.

Altered males and spayed females can also be guilty of spraying, especially if threatened by another cat in the house (or even in the neighborhood). Luckily, this, too, is less common than with intact cats.

For stubborn cases of spraying, your vet may suggest dosages of medroxy-progesterone (MPA), administered to both males (neutered and nonneutered) and females (neutered only).

Cleaning

How to remove urine and feces stains from carpets and furniture is a real problem. Baking soda spread on the wet spot, left to dry, and then vacuumed up, works for some people. White vinegar or chlorine bleach, diluted and used as a scrubbing agent, is also effective, say others. Plain soap and water, flavored with a little ammonia, is my method. And plenty of scrubbing. Commercial products are available at most pet stores. Some people swear by them; others say they are useless.

Be sure you clean the pad *under* the carpet, as well as the carpet itself. Professional cleaning may sometimes be the only answer if the soiling is severe.

*

If your cat has "sprayed" an object in the house, no ordinary cleaning will remove the strong odor. After cleaning, use a commercial cat deodorant like "Rocket Knok" concentrate.

*

If cleaning or deodorants do not work, you may just have to throw away the rug or bath mat or whatever the cat has sprayed. The stink can last forever.

Pica

Occasionally cats, as well as dogs, will suddenly develop an appetite for something not considered fit to eat. This neurosis is called *pica*.

*

Cats may start gnawing on wood or eating cat litter or sand.

*

No one is quite sure why animals feel compelled to ingest that which is indigestible. Nutritional deficiencies are sometimes blamed and should certainly be looked into by you and your veterinarian.

*

The doctor should also examine your cat for worms, hairballs, cancer, and pancreatitis.

*

Another cause may be too-early weaning or an emotional upset. Is there a new pet in the household? A new baby? Look into all aspects of your pet's environment as well as its diet.

*

The commonest form of pica (and one not traceable to any of the above possible causes) is cloth-eating. Although wool is generally preferred (sweaters, argyle socks, blankets), cats have been caught happily swallowing everything from terrycloth towels to chenille bedspreads.

*

For reasons thought to be hereditary, Siamese are by the far the worst offenders. Even cats with a little Siamese in them are much more likely to turn out to be cloth-eaters than other cats. (Siamese are also inclined to be

tail-chewers and paw-suckers—possibly a related neurosis.) A few Siamese seem to outgrow the habit with no therapy. But don't count on it.

Remedies that do *not* seem to work include change of diet, lots of petting, punishment, and even the extreme resort of removing the teeth. (The cat sucks instead of chews.)

Some veterinarians have had luck with offering the cloth-eating cat daily small doses of unscented lanolin, found in most drug stores. (If it doesn't work, it won't hurt the cat.)

Others suggest half a grain of thyroid hormone daily. This should not be tried without veterinary approval.

If neglected, cloth-eating can result in impacted intestines, which is treatable only by surgery.

Why Not a Second Pet?

It is my long-held opinion that two pets are easily four times as much fun as one. And no more trouble.

Perhaps it is because I myself was an only child that I sympathize so easily with single pets, who must spend so much time amusing themselves or, what is worse, allaying boredom by chewing slippers, soiling rugs, scratching furniture, or other similar destructive activities.

While a cat is a creature of routine and can adapt more easily than a dog to long days without companionship (as long as its owner returns at a more-or-less regular hour each evening), it too is more social than most people realize and becomes depressed if left alone too long.

*

The best way to provide a cat with a lifelong best friend is to adopt two kittens in the beginning, usually littermates.

*

If you take kittens of the same sex, you solve certain obvious problems immediately; but if not, you can have them altered later on.

*

Sibling matings are to be discouraged for all sorts of genetic reasons, to say nothing of the pet population explosion.

*

When you introduce a new kitten to older Tabby, be sure to show the latter some special affection, much as you would an older child when you bring the new baby home from the hospital. Eventually the mature animal will usually adopt a protective attitude toward the younger one.

*

Kittens are particularly happy to make friends with just about anybody—if they're introduced cautiously in the beginning.

*

Let your cat make the first overture. It's also a good idea if there's some-place Kitty can climb. She doesn't like to feel cornered.

*

Superstition would have us believe that cats and dogs are natural enemies. But there are many examples of canines and felines who have adopted one another—as foster mothers and babes, as good pals, or at least as mutually accepted members of the same family.

*

Some veterinarians do not accept the idea that there is an instinctual animosity between certain animals. It's their belief—and it's verified by numerous examples—that even grown animals can learn to get along with and accept species other than their own.

*

Suppose you have a lonely Irish Setter who needs a friend. Your household cannot accommodate two romping dogs (maybe you live in a city apartment) but can adjust to a dog and cat. If you decide to bring a kitten into the life of Kelly, your Irish Setter, great care must be exercised.

*

Introductions can best be accomplished by two people—one for each pet.

*

Kelly has sniffed at the door and knows full well that Something is on the other side. Curiosity struggles with fear. Let your friend hold Kelly with a firm grip on his leash while you pick up the kitten and seat yourself across the room.

*

Kitty will probably show little interest, but Kelly may have a Setter-sized fit.

*

Lots of soothing speech and petting are in order for both animals on their first meeting. After a few minutes of sweet talk and cuddling for both animals, put Kitty on the floor but don't let go of her. Let the dog approach, with the leash still held taut by your partner, for a closer look.

*

With most dogs the difference in size between themselves and the kitten is enough to banish any threat, but with some dogs this cannot be counted on.

*

Every encounter of this kind involves a slightly different scenario. Irish Setters are usually of a gentle disposition, however, so let us assume Kelly is now wagging his tail and giving every evidence of detente.

*

Let the animals rub noses.

*

Kitty may hiss, arch her back, and blow up her tail. Pay all this no mind; it is just reflexive defense behavior. But see to it that it doesn't extend to giving Kelly a swipe across the chops just to let him know Kitty is Boss.

*

And she probably will be, despite seniority or discrepancies in sizes.

*

One meeting may be all that is necessary, but in many cases, it is not.

If it seems to you that relations are, at best, a mite strained, separate the two pets again, keeping Kitty in her room with the door securely shut.

*

Kelly, who is used to having the run of the house, should be permitted to continue lording it over his territory, with lots of extra TLC thrown in for good measure.

*

Keep Kitty safely out of the fray (with bed, water, food, and litter pan, of course) and look in on her frequently. She too needs company, attention, and lots of affection in these rather trying first days.

*

In a few hours, repeat the conditioning process. Positive signs on both sides should predominate over the negative. The next day, repeat again if common sense indicates.

*

When you are able to let both pets meet without restraint and when they exhibit playful behavior without signs of mayhem, you can relax your vigil.

*

Keep the pets' feeding areas separate.

*

Keep your eye on both animals for a while. Any kitten is a fragile piece of goods.

*

The advantages of two pets so outweigh any disadvantages that it is hard for me to understand why more families do not give themselves the treat. To watch them play together, groom each other, sleep together (with one making a pillow of the other), is one of the joys of pet ownership.

*

If cat and cat or dog and cat seem too tame a combination for you, your pet may take it into its head to provide its own "best friend."

*

Stories are legion of cats adopting baby skunks, mice, possums, rabbits, fawns, raccoons, and, on farms, becoming chummy with cows, horses, and pigs.

I once almost had a heart attack when I saw my two cats heading for the pet bantam rooster next door. I was halted in mid-sprint when I realized cats and chicken were playing tag with the utmost affability. "Oh, didn't you know?" asked the rooster's owner. "They've been buzzum pals for months. Damndest thing I ever saw!" Buzzum, indeed. The peaceable kingdom in one's own backyard. It sure beats a Pet Rock.

CHAPTER SIX

Owner Relationship and Responsibility

Are You a Dog Person or a Cat Person?

Everyone knows that if you tell a child that cats are dangerous and untrust-worthy, the child will grow up hating cats. Ditto with dogs. Preference in pets usually begins early in life and has to do as much with personality as with conditioning.

*

As for cats and dogs, they do not share many important qualities. So it is good to know which set of personality traits suits you best.

Extrovert Versus Introvert

In general, the more gregarious the person, the greater the likelihood of preferring dogs over cats.

*

Dogs are pack animals; cats are sybarites but loners.

*

A dog must have company—preferably yours, because you are identified as "pack leader" from the time you first impose authority over it.

*

A cat chooses to spend long hours in solitude and becomes sociable only on its own terms. As for authority, the word can't be found in any feline lexicon.

Dependent Versus Independent

A dog is always anxious to please. It is emotionally dependent; it sometimes even fawns.

A cat is independent in the sense of being self-contained, but it is not indifferent. Its signs of love are subtle.

The dog treats you as a master; the cat looks on you as an equal. Not everyone can stand it.

Outdoors Versus Indoors

The natural environment for a dog is outdoors, preferably where it can run freely in an open field or along a beach, even though in our urban world these conditions often do not prevail.

A cat, though it may love its own backyard and familiar trees, is more at home inside the house. It can spend a rich, full life running up and down carpeted cat "trees," climbing into cupboards, chasing catnip mice, and wearing out its favorite chair or bed.

People who prefer hiking, hunting, fishing, or camping in the woods to sitting by the fire with a good book usually prefer dogs to cats.

Active Versus Contemplative

Dogs are bouncy, exuberant animals; cats are quiet. The active person relates to the sudden movements, the jumpings up and down, of a dog. The contemplative person is more at ease with a cat's calm.

Trainable Versus Do It My Way Or Else

If you prefer obedience to rugged individualism, choose a Beagle over a Siamese.

It is much easier to teach a dog than a cat how to live with its human family.

*

An intelligent dog can learn not only the basic commands of obedience training, but infinitely more complex signals.

*

A dog can be trained to do tricks and to perform such undoggy feats as riding a bicycle or tracking down marijuana buried in ten thicknesses of packaging.

*

Cats can indeed be taught to adapt to our lives, but there are always clearly defined limits beyond which any self-respecting cat will not go.

*

Cats can be taught such nonsense as jumping through a hoop or rolling over, but they're better at teaching *you* games.

*

A dog can understand as many as two hundred words—at least, well enough to make the correct responses.

*

Cats seem to recognize the meaning of a few words, especially when they are associated with certain sensory stimuli or particular times of day. "Din-Din!" called at the same time every day is going to elicit a hasty run to the supper dish.

*

Most of the things dogs will do to earn points with their masters, cats consider beneath their dignity, though cats that respond to commands are certainly not unknown.

Straightforward Versus Devious

Cat detractors love to point out that cats are sneaky and devious, while dogs are straightforward, honest, brave, trustworthy, helpful . . . reverent.

*

Cat lovers have a hard time with this, because it is perfectly true that cats are mysterious.

*

A cat is never far away from its jungle ancestry, whereas a dog is much more domesticated.

To watch a cat stalking its prey is to see a miniature tiger ready to pounce and kill. This fact makes some pet owners uneasy, while it intrigues others. Only you know in which group you belong.

Masculine Versus Feminine

Although cat people do not like to admit it, I think there is some truth to the cliché that dogs generally appeal more to men; cats, to women.

*

The common appellation of "she" to cats and "he" to dogs is not without some validity.

*

Women tend to identify with the beauty and grace of cats, with their gentleness and softness, even with their independence.

*

Men seem to admire dogs for their faithfulness and devotion, for their strength and courage.

*

All kinds of crossovers are possible with this generalization, because we all have masculine and feminine aspects to our personalities and because there are many variations among the animals of both species.

*

There are people who love dogs and cats with apparently equal ardor, and more and more families enjoy living with both animals, appreciating the unique qualities of each. Felix and Fido like it too.

How to Communicate with Cats

Communication, like friendship, is a two-way street. If you want to be able to "talk to the animals," you must first listen to what they have to say to you.

*

Cats have several modes of communication. Sometimes they will use one, sometimes another. If you are not hearing them, they will snow you with all systems at once.

Body Language

Every cat has a sign system that perceptive owners learn by heart. Body language is focused in the tail, eyes, and ears, and every cat is both unique to itself and similar to its kind.

140

*

Every cat's tail is slightly different from every other's—plumey, arched forward, kinked like a question mark, and so on—but the way it holds its tail means the same thing for all cats.

*

Held high like a flag means: "I am happy, I am secure, I am king of this house."

*

A cat coming into strange territory, such as a new home, will walk low to the floor, tail down, sniffing out all the corners. When it is satisfied that there is no danger, its whole body will lift and its tail will come up to full mast.

*

A tail lashing back and forth in a cat means it is angry or about to spring. A fat, bristling tail always signals hostility—usually toward another animal.

*

Cats seldom wag their tails.

*

A dragging tail usually translates as illness, fear, or depression.

Ears and Eyes

Cats have expressive ears. They lie down flat when they're angry. They prick up when they're alert and listening.

Watch your cat's ears when you're talking to it behind its back. The ears will swivel, scooping up sound from the air, but its head won't move. And it doesn't miss a thing.

*

Cats' eyes give away feelings too. They can flash with anger, become dark with fear or excitement (the iris filling the cornea), or seem to melt with love.

*

Cats often show affection, too, by slowly closing their eyes to a slit, opening, closing. It is a sight to seduce the most fanatic cat hater.

The Whole Body

A healthy cat either sprawls on its side or on its back, or lies with its paws buttoned up, tail wound round its body. A sleeping, secure animal is a lovely sight.

*

A sick cat will crouch on the floor or in a corner, hunched into the smallest space possible, usually crying, but sometimes ominously still.

*

The familiar arched-like-a-croquet-wicket stance of a cat signifies alarm to even the most obtuse.

*

One of the most appealing (and subtle) postures of a cat is the way it will sit like a jug in front of a door when it wants someone to let it out. Not a peep, not a twitch of a whisker; only the ears are turned like semaphores to the rear.

*

Pure eloquence is the cat's shake of the paw when a new kind of food is dismissed as unworthy.

*

If a cat scratches all around the dish, the food is being labeled fit for burial.

*

Cats read us too. They learn quickly what we mean by hand signals, facial expressions, and body movements.

*

Always be consistent with any communication to your pet. Don't use a signal for one thing on Monday and for another on Tuesday.

Sound

Every housekeeper to cats quickly learns to distinguish between one miaow and another. Although some cats seem to go through life emitting only genteel ejaculations, most felines have a vocabulary equal to all their needs and emotions.

*

Basic Cat is spoken by all members of the species and can be understood by people if they pay attention.

*

I have a cat who is very verbal, who talks all the time in dozens of different modulations. I became well acquainted with most of his glossary through exposure, but the rest I had to learn by diligent attention. My chatty cat has a small, crisp sound which means "Hi!" His long, piercing, peremptory "Me-e-e-uu-w" is his way of saying, "Where's breakfast? I'm starved!" A polite "Mew" means "Thank you" or "Out," or a little of both. When he has caught a mouse, his hunter's cry is unmistakable: "I bring you treasure!" Now and then—if he's in direct confrontation with another cat, for instance—he lets out some "Yow-yow-yows," which are better left untranslated.

*

When a cat's body language and voice are combined, it is hard not to get the message. When Felix jumps into your lap, kneads it to make it his, and purrs like a motorboat, you can be sure he wants a little loving.

*

The kneading process is a hangover from babyhood, when the kitten kneaded its mother to make the milk flow faster. In adulthood, it is plainly a sign of affectionate dependency, if only for the moment.

*

Purring usually denotes happiness, though cats also purr when they are merely agitated, as in a veterinarian's office.

*

Most cats verbalize to other cats only if they're angry or in love.

Touch

A cat can tell us it cares by pushing its head into our hands, placing a paw on our arm or face, rubbing our ankles, or giving us gentle lovebites that don't hurt.

*

In turn we stroke, pet, scratch, rub, hold, and fondle a cat, and thus tell it how much we love it, value its companionship and respect its catness.

✳

In summary, if you want to communicate with your pet, first make sure you understand what he is trying to say to *you*. This is an ongoing process, not something you learn in a week.

✳

Don't just talk baby talk to Felix. He is an individual spirit with a life of his own and a language to match. Talk to him on a horizontal level, not down from your lofty perch to his subservient one. You'll be surprised how much you'll learn.

Cats and ESP

All animals, especially those who live as companions to man, seem to have sixth, seventh, and eighth senses.

✳

Could it be because animals' minds are not as cluttered as ours with "matters of consequence," that they are able to sense rhythms and vibrations we have lost touch with?

✳

The power of clairvoyance, it seems, is particularly sharp in cats. Almost every housekeeper to cats has a story to tell about their mysterious knowing and foreknowing, to which no other animals can hold a candle.

✳

Cats' apparent ability to see things beyond our sight and to hear things we cannot hear has inspired a whole literature on the subject.

✳

My own experience with this sort of thing concerned my husband's cat, Pee Wee, who never failed to anticipate David's arrival home from work, even though the exact time varied. Ten minutes (the exact time of the walk from the commuters' train to the apartment) before my husband's key turned in the lock, Pee Wee would station himself on a small table inside the front door, teetering precariously, craning his neck in anticipation of the arrival.

✳

Clairaudience is a similarly baffling sense. An Abyssinian I know who loathes the sound of the telephone will rouse out of a sleep, fly across the room like one possessed, and knock the receiver off the hook. What makes her psychic is that she often begins her mad dash to the phone *before* it rings.

∗

The stories of cats who can sense loss and feel grief are too numerous to list, contrary to the myth that cats are not attached to their owners.

∗

In their book, *The Strange World of Animals and Pets*, Vincent and Mary Gaddis tell of a well-loved cat in Georgia whose owner was taken to the hospital, where she died. When the family came back from the hospital they found the cat in a state of hysteria, howling her anguish, jumping onto her mistress's bed, and patting the pillow. She seemed to know her mistress wouldn't be back.

∗

Over and over again anecdotes are told of a cat's coming home from a long distance (called appropriately the homing instinct, though no one knows how it is done), and even more remarkable tales are told of cats finding their families in new territories, as though they were part bloodhound instead of all cat. This ability, called psi trailing, has been investigated in some detail by the late Dr. J. B. Rhine, former director of Duke University's Parapsychology Laboratory.

∗

Homing stories are touching examples of both extrasensory perception and loyalty. Take Snowy of Ross, England, who disappeared from his owners' summer holiday house and three months later found his way home, seventy-five miles away, by some sort of tracking device in his catty brain.

∗

Wahoo, who lived in Seattle, was en route to Alaska with his owner. He escaped in British Columbia and eleven months later, his long hair dirty and matted, turned up in Seattle purring with happiness.

∗

Homing is astonishing enough, but what about psi trailing? What possible explanation is there for Pooh of Wellford, South Carolina, for instance, who walked over two hundred miles to rejoin his family in their new home after he had been given to a friend in Newman, Georgia? It took him over a year, but he made it.

∗

In Poughkeepsie, New York, a cat named Sparky was left behind when his family moved to California. Nine months later a cat arrived at the new home in Livermore, a place he had never visited, after traveling across more

145

than three thousand miles of unknown territory. He was skinny and had a sore on his back, but he was unmistakably Sparky, even to the crook in his tail.

*

A famous case of Dr. Rhine's concerned a cat named Clementine. Left behind in Dunkirk, New York, she took off for Denver one day in search of her family, who had left her with neighbors because she was expecting kittens—a reasonable excuse, you might say. Clementine didn't think so. As soon as the kittens were weaned she pointed west, and made it in a little over three months. There was no doubt that it was Clementine on that Denver doorstep, for this incredible animal had seven toes on each front paw, two white spots on her tummy, and a scar on her left shoulder from an old burn. That Clementine survived a journey over mountains and plains was unbelievable enough, but how did she find the one city, street, and house she was aiming for? No one really knows for sure.

*

Psychokinesis (mind over matter) is another branch of ESP in which animals have made their own history. In Los Gatos ("the cats"), near San Jose, California, electronics engineer Ira Spector has perfected a machine to measure psychokinesis (PK) in people and animals.

*

A star subject is Funky, the experimenter's cat, who likes to lie on a heating pad on a cold day. The cat was hooked to the PK meter, which in turn was attached to the heating pad. With the meter set at a random off-and-on rate, the heating pad would turn on 750 times out of 1500 if only chance was operating. Shivering Funky left nothing to chance. Just by "willing it," the cat managed to turn on the pad 820 times, or 70 times more than chance. The odds against this being accidental are 2000 to 1.

Cats and Children

Some children try to treat a cat the way they would Raggedy Ann. There are two solutions: give the cat to a safer owner, or educate the child that a cat is a high-strung animal that needs special handling. Don't use the cat as an object lesson in compassion past the point of common sense. You can damage its nervous system forever, and the child will still be disturbed.

*

Some children seem to have been born loving cats and knowing exactly how to handle them. The far larger majority need to know that a cat is a very special animal—not a dog (who can stand far more punishment), and not a teddy bear.

A Few Pointers

The first thing to teach a child about a cat is how to pick it up. Don't let your little boy or girl grab it by the scruff of the neck the way its mother does. Mother cats know how; people don't.

*

The child should be taught to lift a cat with one hand under its front legs and the other hand supporting the cat's hind legs and bottom. Most children let cats dangle; some drag them around upside down. Either method of transportation is enough to send a cat to a psychiatrist.

*

Cats are so soft, it is tempting to clutch them in a fond embrace and squeeze them. A kitten can be squeezed to death; any adult cat resists restraint of its person and may scratch to get away. If the child always holds Tabby gently and lets her go the minute she shows signs of restlessness, she will soon learn to jump up on the child's lap for a little love-in.

*

Encourage your child to fondle the kitty every day. Cats will cry and pace the floor if they do not get enough affection.

*

Cats hate loud noises, so constantly remind Junior to speak softly to Tabby. A loud "No! No!" should be saved for such misdemeanors as scratching the furniture or swiping the salmon.

*

If you see your child spanking his cat, explain to him that the cat doesn't like it any better than he would and that it doesn't do any good.

*

Don't let your child tease a cat. Teasing can make a cat (and a child) cruel.

*

Don't let young Tommy box with the cat, either. Even kittens can easily be taught to box and seem to enjoy it. The trouble is that in boxing, cats also learn to keep their claws out and learn how to bite. Gentleness and sweetness can also be conditioned.

*

When a cat is eating, tell your youngster to leave it alone. Cats have one-track minds and hate to be petted or talked to when dining. The same goes, double, for when the cat is napping. Cats need lots of sleep—just like babies.

*

147

All of the above is even more important if the cat is a kitten. No kitten under eight weeks old should be entrusted to a child. Even with a two-month-old, strict supervision is essential.

If ground rules are carefully observed, cats make wonderful pets for children. The combination of a well-brought-up cat and a well-brought-up child makes a happy friendship for both.

What Children Can Really Learn from Pets

Dennis, seven years old and the middle child of a large family, was so sullen and withdrawn that his parents finally took him to a psychologist for advice. Among other things, the therapist prescribed a pet that would belong to Dennis alone. After a look around at the local humane society, Dennis went home with his very own calico cat. End of story? Happy.

This small case history is repeated over and over across the country, and illustrates what most children (and parents) can testify to concerning the healing and educational qualities of pet ownership.

What is the give and take between pets and children?

Companionship

Childhood can be a mighty lonely place, no matter how many people occupy the same home.

To Dennis, the cat he named Patches became an intimate part of his world. She slept on his bed at night; she was waiting for him when he came home from school; and when an overly solicitous father didn't notice, sat on his lap during breakfast and dined on leftover cereal afterwards.

My own first cat played a similar role. I even dressed her up in doll clothes and wheeled her around the neighborhood in the buggy. She didn't mind anything, including being ignored. I, an only child, had a built-in sibling who purred, rubbed against me, liked being stroked and fondled, and who apparently loved me as much as I loved her. Furthermore, unlike my mother, she was totally uncritical.

While the cat, unlike the dog, never gives one the assurance of one's superiority, it will always treat you as an equal. Not all adults can qualify on that score.

Responsibility

Although Dennis was only seven (a good age for pet responsibility—under six is usually too young), his mother gave him full domain over Patches, with only unobtrusive supervision to see that the cat did not suffer neglect and that Dennis did not carry her around upside down.

*

Dennis was told to get a book on cat care, and together he and his mother figured out the important points.

*

Obviously there were going to be differences between the care given to Patches and that already well established for Max, the family dog, to whom Dennis had always been indifferent.

*

Dennis fed Patches every morning before breakfast, gave her a quick brushing, and changed the litter pan. When he got home from school he checked to see if the pan needed changing again. After that he was free to do as he liked until it was time for the evening meal.

*

Dennis began to pay much more attention to Max after Patches became a member of the family. After all, it was the boy's job to introduce the two animals in such a way that Max didn't scare the spots off the cat, or, as was more likely, that Patches didn't take a lethal swipe at Max's sensitive schnoz.

*

With a little help from his brothers, Dennis managed this satisfactorily. While a child is so dependent on adults, a pet is dependent on *him*. Pet ownership can let a child practice growing up.

Biological Realities

The old theory that a cat—or a dog, rabbit, or what have you—should be allowed to breed so that children can learn the facts of life, has been replaced by the much more practical idea that there are enough unwanted animals in the world to make neutering and spaying of pets a virtual necessity.

*

Even that bit of surgery, however, can be educational. ("Why can't Tabby have kittens?")

149

Many children hate to eat what is good for them. The fact that his pet is given a diet rich in the proper nutrients may impress a young owner that he should drink his milk, eat his vitamins, and stop yammering about it.

Good elimination habits are taken matter-of-factly in the pet world, but if Tabby makes a mistake on the living room carpet, Junior is not going to lose face by cleaning it up.

Naps and quiet are prescribed for animals as well as kids, and if shared, do not seem other than routine.

When a pet is sick, it must be taken to the doctor and often cared for at home with pills or other medical procedures looked upon with loathing by the child but endured by both child and animal, with proper persuasion.

Values, Etc.:

Although it is certainly true that some children treat their pets with lack of consideration, not to say downright cruelty, there is usually something very wrong in the total emotional environment of such children (sometimes even parental abuse); such abuse is not, I believe, the outcome of normal child-pet interaction.

Most children learn from handling their pets countless attributes that can influence larger areas of their lives.

Children learn to *empathize* with their charges, or if they and their animals are at odds, to make judgments as to which one of them will prevail in a given situation or conflict.

*

Compassion when Tabby has the sniffles lets a child bestow on a pet the same tenderness that is given him by his parents in similar situations.

*

A child, usually heedless at best, learns early the values of **gentleness** and *patience* in the care of a pet.

*

Loyalty is another quality highly valued by the owner of a pet. Although dogs may exhibit this trait more overtly, it is also apparent in cats.

*

A sense of proportion also stands high on my list, as I remember how close to the natural rhythm of life my cats have always lived. They enjoyed simple pleasures such as chasing a Ping-Pong ball or a leaf. They slept when they were tired, played when they were frisky. They knew where to find warmth and comfort, and where and when to seek solitude.

*

The loss of a pet brings its own poignant lessons in how to bear separation. I wept buckets at nine when my first cat had to be given away, but I survived. When another cat had to be "put to sleep" (a euphemism that has always bothered me), a part of me seemed to die with him. But I survived that too.

*

Perhaps more than any other quality, pets teach children the sense of the "other."

*

Naturally egocentric, a child learns that someone else—an animal with whom he cannot communicate just with words—has a life style of its own, wishes and needs of its own, and sometimes instincts of the wild that cannot be imprinted with those of the child.

*

A friend's granddaughter, Becky, had come into the kitchen just as her cat Jefferson was polishing off the remains of a rabbit caught in the meadow nearby and brought in through the cat door. Becky's mother hustled the cat and his prey out the back door, but not before four-year-old Becky had taken in the whole scene. Arms akimbo, she looked down at the floor covered with rabbit fuzz, shook her head, and said with the wisdom of a small Buddha: "Well, *I* don't like this at all, but *Jefferson* does!"

*

(For indoor-outdoor cats, it seems on first glance to be a great idea to give your cats a door of their own for easy coming and going. Long ago I had to give up the cat door in my house and go back to being doorwoman for my pets. The reasons were simple: my cats brought into the house not only themselves but the half-dead birds and mice they had caught; and neighbors' cats followed the leader and dropped in to steal my cats' food.)

Safety

Our modern life, complete with every kind of electrical appliance and chemical helpmate, was not designed with Puss in mind. It is up to you to keep your cat safe from accidents.

Watch your open-door policy with a cat around the house. Its natural love affair with small enclosed spaces will lead it into dresser drawers, cupboards, refrigerators, even file cases—into *C* for cat—if left open. Shut the door without looking and it's the cat's miaow, loud but muffled.

The cat's craving for cozy places can even be the death of it. A cat curled up in the washing machine will never make it through the rinse cycle. Keep washers shut—also dryers.

The kitchen is probably the most hazardous, and the most attractive, room in the house to your feline, especially during meal preparation. Small kittens are easily stepped on in the traffic between sink and stove. Even big cats, weaving in and out between ankles, hoping for a handout, are in danger of ending up with wounded toes or tail. Keep your cat out of the kitchen during mealtime by feeding it in its own out-of-the-way corner first.

A cat's natural instinct to snitch any tasty morsels within leaping distance insures that a cat in your kitchen means, eventually, a cat on the stove. Scorched fur and burned paw pads, can be avoided by excluding Puss from meal preparation.

In the stove is no good either. Keep the oven door closed or Puss could be baked with the muffins. (I know of one who was and survived, but it didn't do him any good.)

A cook can also spill the beans or boiling-hot soup by tripping over a cat who shouldn't be in the kitchen.

*

Watch those tasty twines used in tying roasts and fowl. Tantalized, Tabby might swallow one. Result: possible serious damage to her gastrointestinal tract and an emergency trip to the veterinarian.

*

Carefully dispose of fish or chicken bones, which choke a cat.

*

The area under the kitchen sink containing cleaners, polishes, bleaches, and so on, is also off limits to cats. Keep the bottles tightly closed and the door shut.

*

If you have a swinging door in your house, be careful that Tabby doesn't get caught in the back swing.

*

Bathrooms have their own hazards. Small kittens have fallen into toilets or tubs and drowned. Keep the lid of the toilet down. If you are drawing a bath, shut the door.

*

All bathroom chemicals poisonous to cats must be stored out of Tabby's reach in unbreakable, airtight containers. These include antiperspirants, nail polish remover, home permanent solutions, hair dyes, hair removers, suntan lotion, detergents and all cleaning fluids, and any chemical containing phenol.

*

A common line of phenol-based products used in bathrooms is advertised for deodorizing a cat's litter box. I would never use it for that purpose, despite the promotion. (If you must, the spray form is the *least* toxic.)

*

If one of the organophosphate strips sold at supermarkets to repel flying insects is hung in a small room where Tabby hangs out, it can give her nausea and possible long-term problems. In fact, bug off the unsparing use of all insecticides in your home if you want a healthy cat.

*

Signs of chemical poisoning are drooling and nausea. Get the cat to a vet pronto.

*

A spool of thread is an all-time favorite cat's play. Tabby is not particular, though, as to whether the thread she has found in your sewing basket has a needle attached to it—and it's highly dangerous if swallowed. Keep your sewing box tightly shut.

*

Crayons, cigarettes, and matches also make tempting toys, but are dangerous if chewed.

*

Don't let Tabby chew on electric cords for fear of shocking results. If you find your cat knocked out, pull the cord from the socket *before* you touch the animal. Then call the vet—fast.

*

Common houseplants can be deadly to your cat. Philodendron, poinsettia, dieffenbachia, elephant's ears, and hyacinths are among the commoner indoor poisonous plants tempting to the cat. Cats have also been caught nibbling on toxic *plastic* greenery. Either hang such plants beyond the cat's paw—and teeth—or get rid of them entirely.

*

Outdoor plants poisonous to cats are, chiefly, lily of the valley, azalea, Castor bean, daffodil, oleander, rhododendron, narcissus bulb, laurel, jimson weed, ivy, and jasmine. Frankly, I confess that my garden contains many of these, and my cats have never paid any attention to them!

*

Snail bait is, of course, very poisonous to cats. I avoid it, even though I dislike snails.

*

If your cat should be poisoned, the commonest symptom is vomiting, frequently accompanied by diarrhea. The cat may not be able to stand without wobbling. Convulsions are common, as are frothing and foaming around the mouth. Other symptoms may be rapid breathing and wild behavior, such as running into walls. Unconsciousness may follow quickly. Rush to a veterinarian, who will administer antidotes and supportive therapy.

*

Peril is also parked in the family garage. The cat, for reasons known only to itself, loves the taste of highly toxic antifreeze solution (ethylene glycol) which tends to collect in a pool under the car in winter weather.

*

If the family driver has a habit of leaving the hood open, beware. Without knowing a spark plug from a catnip ball, cats adore crawling into engines for a peek and maybe to sleep. They have also been unwound from axles, radiators, air filters, engine blocks, and transmissions; lifted from under fenders, tire wells, and wheels. Keep the garage door closed and the car's hood down.

*

Holidays can be especially hazardous times. For Tabby, "The First Noel" may well be the last. All kinds of feline hazards come in those fancy Christmas packages hung enticingly from the tree or decking the festive halls. A little forewarning, some caution, and common sense can prevent a lot of heartache and suffering, especially for your new kitten or cat. The older cat may have learned its lesson on Christmases past, but better keep an eye on it, just in case.

*

If you want to keep your *Tannenbaum* upright, keep Tabby out of the branches. Cats also go mad for tinsel, lights, colored balls, and artificial snow. They've been known to chew the wires and ornaments and to swallow the tinsel and snow.

*

The results of these Christmas pastimes can range from unpleasant to fatal. Chewing wires can produce electric shock. Trying to teethe on ornaments that splinter on contact can cause perforated gastric or intestinal walls.

*

Metallic icicles have a peculiar fascination for cats, and many are the times that feline pet owners have had to pull soggy strands of the stuff from a gagging cat's throat. If swallowed, icicles and tinsel can cause paralyzed innards.

*

Artificial snow is poisonous; cotton is almost as bad.

*

Keep a sharp eye on Puss when you are opening Christmas presents. Ribbon, cord, and string make a tempting meal. Constipation is only one of the minor ailments that can result. The swallowed string or ribbon can become wrapped around the bowel and strangle it.

*

Even worse than string is rubber—one of the principal causes for surgery at this time of year. Check those toys you plan to give your cat and be sure they are not of foam rubber, but of sturdier stuff that cannot be chewed into tiny bits.

*

Cellophane has a fascinating crackling sound, but when swallowed, develops hardened cutting edges that injure your cat's tummy.

*

Keep small objects out of reach of your cat. Other swallowables that can be lethal are small toys, flash bulbs, matches, needles, aluminum foil, and pipe cleaners.

*

There are other perils, the greatest of which has to be crowds and their attendant evils: people coming and going, doors opening and closing, often left open. Results: pets stepped on, pets lost.

*

Despite your watchful eye, what if something goes wrong? Say Tabby gets a bone in her throat or munches on a small toy. There are some positive things you can do while you wait for the veterinarian. If the object is still in the throat, force the mouth open by pressing with thumb and forefinger on either side of the cheeks. If you see an object, gently reach in and remove it; act quickly but don't force. If this method doesn't work, press the palm of your hand firmly into the abdomen of your pet, just below the rib cage. With the palm of your other hand maintain constant pressure on the lower abdomen. The object should pop right out.

*

Never try to remove a needle; that is a job for the veterinarian.

*

Another common visitor in the pet stomach at Christmastime arrives via the holiday fowl. If your pet hasn't tried to swallow the twine trussing the turkey or goose, it's the bone, wing, thigh, or whatever. Be particularly careful in disposing of the remains of the feast.

*

Give your pet its own Christmas dinner from a nice safe can. It will be better nourished and in no danger from choking on a brittle bone. As a matter of fact, you can even find turkey in a cat food these days. Just the thing for a Merry, Merry!

*

Overfeeding is a problem for pets as well as people. And, unfortunately, the table carries nothing of value for Tabby, from the stuffed olives to the mince pie and assorted nuts. There is a lot, on the contrary, that can make her pretty sick: candied yams, smoked oysters, and brandied eggnog. So please, when dinnertime comes, make it a loud and clear "No, no!" Otherwise, Tabby may end up with a bad case of the blahs or worse.

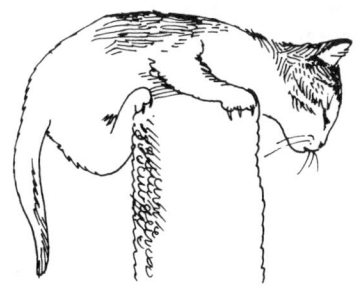

*

Deck the halls with caution: keep plant decorations out of your cat's reach. Be particularly careful with poinsettia and holly berries. Both are poisonous to some degree to cats.

*

As for mistletoe, it's the most poisonous of all. Hang it high. Dispose of dropped berries immediately. (It is just as poisonous to your pet pooch.) And don't hold your cat up to look at it. If you must kiss your feline favorite, try it someplace else!

*

In a case of poisoning, give an emetic right away. Try two teaspoons of hydrogen peroxide or salt or one tablespoon of mustard powder to a cup of warm water orally every five minutes until vomiting occurs.

*

One more thing. You may have noticed how hard it is to find a kitten for Christmas. For reasons known only to nature, cats seldom give birth to kittens that are ready for weaning by Christmas. Maybe sometime long ago they saw what was coming and determined to boycott the whole business.

Tips for Moving With Cats

If you expect to move this year—as do an estimated forty-five million Americans—make sure you include your cat in the list of "Things to take care of."

*

Cats have been known to pack themselves into the moving van and turn up in their new homes after being confined for miles without food, water, sandbox, or catnip.

*

Owners can avoid moving-day trauma for both themselves and their cat if they do a little planning beyond considering how the crystal goblets are to be packed and where to stash Grandma's rocking chair.

*

Long before the cartons move in and the draperies come down, Felix will sense change and begin to get edgy.

*

Keep your cat away from the packing scene as much as possible. If you shut Felix in a spare room with his litter pan, food and water dishes, and toys, he won't be in danger of being trampled underfoot or packed with the Limoges.

*

Some people in the throes of moving have even boarded their cats for fear they will bolt the scene. Most pet owners, however, with careful planning and common sense, can handle their animals during the premoving hullabaloo.

If You're Moving Out of Town

How is Felix going to travel to his new home? If the distance is great, he is probably going to be shipped by air. If you are going to drive and the destination is not too far away, he may be able to travel with you, provided you can make a place for him in the car and he is a good traveler. (See "The Traveling Cat.")

*

If you're moving out of town, it makes good sense for you and Felix to pay a farewell visit to the veterinarian for his checkup, booster shots (many states require rabies inoculation), and interstate health certificate.

*

The interstate health certificate, a must for most interstate transportation, includes a complete description of your pet, a list of all inoculations it has had, and a statement that it is free of all contagious diseases.

*

Some states require receipt of the health certificate as a prerequisite for entry of the pet.

*

At Felix's premoving visit, ask your veterinarian for the name of a colleague in your new city with whom you can check in after you have gotten settled.

*

If a tranquilizer is going to be needed for your cat, obtain it from the veterinarian, with complete instructions for administering it. Do this well in advance of the move. Some veterinarians like to see how the cat reacts to the drug.

The Big Day Dawns

Moving day itself is the time for extreme precautions. If you don't want Felix to take to the hills in sheer panic, make sure he is either confined in a room out of the traffic or boarded in a kennel until the madness has lifted.

If the cat is going with you by automobile, its "luggage" should be stowed away in the car the night before so it is not inadvertently swept up by the movers.

If by some accident your pet should escape and run away in the confusion, don't lose your head. When everyone else has gone and the house is quiet, if empty, you can probably lure him back by calling him, putting out food, and behaving as though it were an ordinary day and you expected him to come home for supper.

This maneuver to lure Felix back to the empty house will work to the degree (1) he is trained to come in at night and (2) he hasn't figured out he is in for a Dislocating Experience. Prevention is much the better idea.

After Arrival

There are many myths about how to orient your pet to his new surroundings. Putting butter on a cat's paw is one of the greasiest and least effective.

All Felix needs is a little time to become accustomed to his new home. Don't let him out for several days. Not even if he pleads and stamps his feet.

What your cat needs most of all at the new address is its own place with the familiar blanket and bed, its litter pan conveniently nearby, its food and water dishes where they can be found without a road map, and lots of reassurance.

Don't be so busy unpacking that you neglect to tell Felix that everything is all right. To him, the whole world has been shaken upside down and *nothing* is right.

When all is calm once more, make an appointment with the vet your doctor told you about. Remember, if you should need the vet in an emergency, you may not be able to get an appointment without first establishing a client relationship.

*

For details of state regulations and requirements on pet transportation as well as advice on moving horses, birds, tropical fish, and other fauna, send to United Van Lines, One United Drive, Fenton, Mo. 63026, for their free booklet, "Moving With Pets."

*

If Felix is traveling by air freight, call the cargo department of whatever airline serves your destination and make arrangements well ahead of time.

*

Don't ship your cat in the hottest time of day during summer months.

*

Airlines and moving companies provide traveling crates (for a fee) to which you will attach names, addresses, and telephone numbers appropriate to the places of origin and destination.

*

Make sure the person who is to receive Felix on the other end is clearly instructed on time and place of arrival.

*

Do not feed your cat within six hours of flying time, but give it small amounts of water.

*

As with land travel, ask your veterinarian about tranquilizers.

The Traveling Cat

Whether you're driving your cat across country or across town to the veterinarian's, it must be kept in its place—in a sturdy, roomy, well-ventilated carrier.

*

The best carrier opens from the top, with sturdy locks and look-through screen panels at each end; cats like to look out. It must be big enough so your cat can stretch out comfortably in it, and made of strong enough material to resist scratching.

Most cats make unsafe back-seat drivers. Left free to wander around the car, they're likely to leap on you at the wrong time—when you're passing another car, for instance. Better a carrier than a harrier.

*

The exceptions to this rule are the cats that have been trained to travel by car from kittenhood. Even these should be collared and leashed en route to avoid losing them at a rest stop.

*

Tabby's going tripping in the family car? First stop should be at the veterinarian's for a checkup, booster shots for feline enteritis, rabies, and other inoculations the doctor thinks necessary.

*

Be sure to ask the veterinarian for health documents to prove that Tabby has had the proper inoculations in case proof is needed.

*

A medical kit for the cat is a useful travel accessory. Your veterinarian can give you advice on its contents. Probably included will be Petromalt to take care of hairballs, diarrhea pills, antibiotic ointment, and, perhaps, tranquilizers.

*

Will your cat check in at a motel en route? If your trip involves overnight stays, inquire of the auto club which hostelries take pets, and make a reservation ahead of time.

*

For longer tripping, you'll want "Touring with Towser," which lists six thousand hotels and motels in the United States that accommodate pets. The booklet can be obtained for one dollar from "Touring with Towser," Dept. WD, Box 1007, Kankakee, Ill. 60901.

*

Pack for the cat. A commodious canvas bag will do. Into it you should pack: plenty of newspapers to line the carrier, a litter box and enough litter for the duration; a favorite blanket and catnip toys; a thermos of cool water; a mop-up towel; canned food and a can opener; a package of dry food; food and water dishes; a steel comb; aforesaid medical kit; and health documents.

*

Feed Tabby two hours before leaving by car and see that she uses her litter pan.

*

161

En route be alert at gas stations and rest stops when Tabby could take to the hills as soon as someone opens the door. Either keep her in the carrier or take her for a walk if she's collar- and leash-trained.

*

To minimize car sickness for touring Tabby, place her carrier on the floor. And line the bottom with newspapers—they're cooler than a towel, and disposable. Place her litter pan beside it, to be offered en route.

*

Do not offer food en route unless it is a long day—and then only dry food. Do offer water, frequently if it is a warm day.

*

If you *must* leave the cat in the car, park in the shade. Open all the windows at least two inches and return within twenty minutes. In warm weather, an unventilated car can heat up to 120 degrees in a very short time, causing heat stroke or death to the cooped-up creature inside.

*

Tabby's carrier turns into her bed for the night at the pets-welcome motel. Let sleeping cats lie in the bathroom with a fresh litter box next to the carrier, and the water dish nearby.

*

Keep the windows locked in the room if you have Tabby in it alone, and post a note on the door that a cat is inside. The maid will appreciate it.

By Air

It can be up, up, and away for Tabby too. If you want your cat to join the jet set with you, check with your airline or travel agent.

*

Some domestic airlines will permit one pet per passenger class if it's small enough to fit in an underseat carrier. If you must ship your cat, call your airline well in advance for guidelines on containers and required health documents.

*

If you go abroad, chances are that once you check on various international regulations for pet visitors, you'll decide to leave Tabby in the good old USA. For instance, all pets must go into a six-month quarantine before they can set paw in Great Britain.

162

By Train

Amtrak does not allow a pet to be shipped by train, either in the passenger compartment or in the baggage compartment. A few years ago this was not so, but humane societies protested the unheated condition of the baggage compartments, and Amtrak decided NO PETS was the best policy.

By Bus

Ditto for Greyhound and Trailways, neither of which will accept a feline passenger.

By Ship

Regulations vary with the line. Some ships have special kennel areas; others do not want to be bothered. Inquire of steamship officials before you include Tabby in your plans.

Leaving the Cat Behind

There is a fine line between responsibility for our pets and overprotectiveness. Although this is an individual distinction, some advice can be given to owners that may relieve their anxiety.

*

It is perfectly okay, for instance, to leave your cats overnight once in a while, provided you leave plenty of food and water for them, and more than one clean litter pan. This does not apply to kittens; only to adult cats.

*

I have a friend who rushes home before 5:00 P.M.—no matter what she is doing or where she is—so her two cats will be fed precisely at the same time every day. This is nonsense. Cats can survive a postponed supper with perfect poise.

*

Weaned kittens are another matter entirely. They demand four to six feedings a day, depending on age, and close supervision.

*

If you are a cat owner and want to take a trip, you don't have to stay home, pawholding. The alternatives are several, depending on the length of time you expect to be away and the temperament of the cat.

There's no place like home for Tabby when you go out of town. Hating change, she's happiest by her own hearth and food dish, well filled.

If you know an intelligent, loving, and highly responsible boy or girl in your neighborhood, offer him or her a cat-tending job while you're away *for a short time*. Clear written instructions (which have been discussed ahead of time) should be left with the child AND the parents.

Explain to the child how important a little petting and play are. Most cats don't care much for the lonely hours between feedings.

A cat-loving older neighbor interested in earning a few dollars would make an ideal drop-in custodian.

In many communities professional pet sitters are available to tend to Tabby while you are away. They can be an excellent solution or a poor one. Get references ahead of time, and leave precise instructions with your house key.

The best stay-at-home plan of all for your cat is to have a trusted friend or relative move in, lock, stock, and love-that-cat. For any pet, home is where human beings live too.

When you take off from Tabby with a custodian in charge, make sure your cat-supply shelf is well filled. In fact, overstock food and other essentials like litter in case you're delayed on your return home.

As you buy last-minute items, pick up a few toys for left-behind Tabby. Her sitter can dole them out, one at a time.

*

Be sure to leave Tabby's doctor's number in plain sight for her keeper, in case she gets sick while you're out of town.

*

If Tabby must be boarded in your absence, ask cat buffs to recommend their favorite kennels. Good cat kennels are not always easily come by. They come in three kinds: the privately owned commercial type, the breeder owned, and the veterinary hospital.

*

Don't leave Tabby at the veterinarian's while you're out of town unless the doctor has a separate wing for boarding pets. Cats will pick up airborne infections from sick animals faster than you can say "Kerchoo."

*

Check out the kennel ahead of time. Any reputable kennel owner welcomes visitors. If inspection is not permitted, go elsewhere.

*

Aside from obvious standards of cleanliness (use your nose as well as your eyes), four essentials should be insisted upon.

*

The first is *safety*. A cat's instinct in captivity is to bolt. Cages—no matter how luxurious—that are kept in backyards without additional safeguards are hazards for boarding cats. The minute the door is opened to admit food and water, the cat may take off for points unknown. Cages must be housed in either a wire enclosure or in a building where the outer barriers will block escape.

*

The second essential is a high-quality diet. Cats in kennels are inclined to be more finicky than usual, so what they have must be *good*. Ask for details. If you prefer, you may bring Tabby's regular food, but don't expect a reduction in fee. It is extra trouble for the kennel attendants.

*

The third requirement is an exercise run. Cats should not be boxed in— they need to stretch their legs. Both health and morale require it, especially if you are going to be gone a couple of weeks.

*

The last—but not least—essential is a concerned and loving attitude on the part of the kennel operators. Cats are too sensitive to be left with uncaring attendants.

Before you take your cat in to be boarded, make sure it has been groomed, has had all its inoculations and boosters (especially FVR), and that your veterinarian's name and phone number are left with the owner in case of an emergency.

Also, write down any medical or behavior history you think important, such as allergies, skin problems, drinks a lot of water, easily startled, etc.

A couple of toys and a familiar blanket are much appreciated while you are away.

The Handicapped Cat

Cats, as well as dogs, sometimes suffer handicaps that make them special objects of affection and care. An automobile accident, for instance, can result in a severed limb. Don't opt for euthanasia; we know several cats that do very well on three legs. Their tripod existence in no way slows down their locomotion, and if they look a little strange, that is a people problem, not a feline one.

Other cats have been known to have epilepsy, necessitating daily medication. As long as they get their pills, they behave as normally as cats without bizarre brain waves,

Cats may also have diabetes (though it is not as common as in dogs), necessitating daily injections of insulin; or heart trouble, requiring regular doses of digitalis. Both become part of the automatic care of the pet.

Some white cats with blue eyes are deaf all their lives. Older cats may have deafness thrust upon them. To test deafness in your cat, use a variety of stimulants that cover a wide frequency: clap your hands, speak, rattle keys, shake the food box, blow a whistle. And be sure the cat can't *see* the source of the sound. Owners of deaf cats must learn also how to attract their pets' attention (stomping on the floor usually does it) and how to give hand signals rather than verbal ones. It is amazing how quickly owner and pet adapt themselves to the situation.

*

Once in a while a cat suffers from blindness, either as a result of trauma or old age. A blind cat can do very well in a house if the owner does not shift the furniture around. It learns its routes, where its bed and food bowls are, where the favorite chair is located, and never runs into anything. Whiskers help.

Sometimes the handicap is orthopedic. Although dachshunds and other low-slung dogs are more frequently the victims of slipped discs or paralysis, cats occasionally join the ranks. A cat named Flip-Flop recently made the news in Boston by getting around without help in a "stroller," custom-made by a group of imaginative carpenters at the Mansfield Training School, where Flip-Flop's owner worked in Occupational Therapy. The device had four wheels, a resting place for Flip-Flop's chin, and support on three sides. Once inside it, he can go any place he wants to except under the bed.

If you keep your sympathies in check but don't extinguish them, if you are empathetic but not sentimental, you will handle the problems of the handicapped cat successfully. The secret is not to become so overprotective that the poor animal becomes an invalid. Keep a consistent routine and your cat will be able to depend on it and you for safety and self-confidence. Don't forget verbal reassurance and petting.

If Your Cat is Lost

If your cat is an indoor-outdoor cat, it may someday disappear. Short-term disappearances are not to be worried about—Miss Puss is probably sleeping under a bush and does not want to be disturbed. Or she is stalking a grass-hopper and has turned off her hearing aid. Or she is on top of the carport contemplating the Ultimate Meaning or What's For Dinner. Be patient and wait for mealtime. She will saunter in.

If Miss Puss is missing inside the house and you have hunted high and low, try looking "in." Open drawers, cupboards, baskets, the piano, are all ideal snoozing areas. Never leave the house with your cat unaccounted for. Especially if the cat is a kitten. It could be in a spot which is not safe for any length of time. Drawers haven't much air. (See "Safety.")

Long-term disappearances are much more dangerous. If your cat has not come home by dinnertime, start hunting immediately. Don't wait. Every minute is precious. Patrol the garden first, calling Miss Puss by name. Then broaden the search to the next-door yard. Keep calling.

If she responds to the sound of the dry food rattling in its box, take the box along and rattle it as you call. Go up and down the street, then back to the house to see if she has sneaked home in your absence.

Repeat this search for at least an hour. Then call your immediate neighbors and report Miss Puss as missing. Keep up the calling at your back door or wherever she was accustomed to go in and out. She may be playing games, but she should return soon because she is presumably hungry.

If she is not back home by bedtime, you can be pretty sure Miss Puss is not being coy—she is lost. There are many possibilities, none of them very happy:

She has been cat-napped. Purebreds are the usual targets, but even Plain Jane Tabby has been known to be taken away by some small child who couldn't resist her furry appeal. If you're lucky, Mother may trace her child's newfound pet back to origin. Or she may let the cat out, and Puss will find her own way home. But there's only a slim chance of that happening. Your best bet is to inquire of all the neighbors (especially those with children) for several blocks around, taking with you a photograph of your cat. Don't rely on verbal description. Most people can't tell the difference between a Siamese-cross and a full-blooded Persian.

Some cat-nappers are professional thieves. (If your cat is a beautiful pure-bred, this kind of theft is a distinct possibility.) If personal calls have been to no avail, run an ad in your local newspaper and in papers of nearby towns, with a full description and an offer of a reward, but don't specify how much. If someone answers, let a middleman handle the negotiations to avoid being ripped off.

Also, it is important to enlist the help of all the older children in your neighborhood. They are not usually potential cat-nappers—it's only toddlers who don't know better. Many of these children may be familiar with your pet. They often prove to be excellent pet finders—conscientious, imaginative, not easily discouraged. You may even offer a small reward, though this is not essential. Most children are animal lovers and will work for free.

*

Mailmen and paper boys are also good candidates for the hunt, especially if they have become friendly with your cat in the course of their appointed rounds.

*

Put up big signs, "CAT MISSING," with its picture and a description, on trees and telephone poles. Also, tack up similar signs on bulletin boards at local supermarkets, schools, and post offices. Be sure to include a telephone number where you can be reached at all times.

*

Another possibility, of course, is that your cat has been hit by a car. Cats are easily spooked by headlights, and if allowed out at night, can freeze in front of a passing car and be instantly killed. If, in searching the streets around your home, not omitting the gutters and curbs, you have not found your cat, inquire of whatever agency is responsible for picking up dead animals. This may be the animal regulation department. They should be able to tell you if a cat was picked up in your area, and what it looked like.

*

If none of these methods have produced results and Miss Puss is still missing, it is time to visit the local animal shelters. Don't rely on an inquiry by phone. Pounds and shelters are terribly busy and cannot check out the fine points of a pet's markings, gender, and age for every distraught owner who calls in. After you have checked out the current occupants, leave with the people in charge a photograph of your cat, a complete description, and your name and telephone number. Then go back every few days for a personal look.

*

While all this is going on, don't stop hunting in your own neighborhood. Cats usually do not wander very far unless they are toms and hunting for females. Any closed-off space, such as a crawl hole under the house or an open window in the garage, should be investigated—not once, but often. Keep calling and scouting. The cat may just be frightened and is longing to be found.

*

If all else fails—or even before you are sure it has—try one of the hot lines for a service that maintains a list of lost-and-found animals. If there is a Pet Patrol system in your town, sponsored by the American Humane Association, you can advertise your loss over the radio free of charge.

*

Rescue and Recovery is a new twenty-four-hour nationwide network for locating lost pets. To join the program, pet owners complete an application covering the pet's vital statistics and medical history, friends or relatives to contact if the owner cannot be located, and authorization for temporary boarding and veterinary care. The owners then receive, for their pet, identification tags bearing their own name and phone number and instructions for contacting the Rescue-and-Recovery service at a toll-free number. In emergencies the service arranges veterinary care and boarding. Cost is ten dollars the first year and five dollars for each year thereafter. For details, write: Fortunate Pet, Inc., P.O. Box 5604, Charlottesville, Va. 22903.

Pet Switchboard, in Shingle Springs, California, has a set-up whereby for a fee of fifteen dollars (good for the lifetime of the animal), you can register your pet and receive a PS collar tag inscribed with the organization's twenty-four-hour-a-day toll-free number: 800-824-5120. In Southern California, another agency engaged in a similar occupation is called Petfinders. A registration fee of twenty dollars includes a number, a tattoo, and a 68 percent success rate of pets returned to owners. Their hot-line number is 213-980-4606.

While you are hunting, think of what preventive measures you may have overlooked. An altered cat is far less likely to wander afield than an unaltered one. Spay and neuter your cat and she or he will tend to stay near home.

A break-away collar with an identification tag is a great idea for an indoor-outdoor cat if the cat doesn't object to it. Some cats don't take to collars. Be sure the collar is either elasticized or will break open if jerked. Cats can become hung up only too easily by leather or plastic collars with no "give."

Tattooing is another means of identification, though it's more popular with dogs than with cats. If you are in favor of it, talk to your veterinarian, who is the best-qualified person for such a job. The inside of a flank is usually used, and if the animal is not a show cat, this is perfectly okay.

Aside from keeping the cat indoors at all times, the best prevention of all—and it isn't 100 percent foolproof—is to let your cat out only when you are with it. At the very least, only do this when you are at home, and check on the cat often. It has a schedule and routine, just as you do. NEVER LET YOUR CAT OUT AFTER DARK. Cats are nocturnal by nature, and they will become intoxicated with the dark if you let them out.

How to Photograph Your Cat

It is perfectly possible to take clear, charming photos of your cat with the most rudimentary box camera. Or an instamatic. Or the most complex of reflex cameras on a tripod.

Whatever you have and are comfortable with, be sure you understand how it works, what its limitations are, when you can use natural light, and when you need a flash. Use it often enough so you don't have to read the instruction manual before each shot. Most importantly, keep it handy and loaded.

An electronic flash that is held to reflect off the ceiling will prevent the light from being mirrored in the animal's eyes (the well-known "red-eye" effect). With an instamatic, the newer flip-flash, which is mounted higher than the older "magic cubes," works very well too.

If your cat spooks every time you aim the camera in its direction, you will have to train it ahead of time before actual shooting takes place. Try accustoming it to the sight and sound of the camera by clicking away at odd moments with no film in the camera. In no time Miss Puss will give it the ho-hum treatment.

The name of the game in all photography is patience and more patience. Dogs can be trained to sit-stay on command, but no cat alive will pose for you just because you're in the mood, the light is behind you, and he is stalking a lizard. If you know your cat's habits well, you can sneak up on it, napping or eating or playing, and catch it in a typical posture.

*

In other words, the most important thing to remember is: don't try to coerce a cat. Inveigle.

*

Certain props and tricks can also be helpful. Holding the camera in one hand and snapping your fingers with the other, you can often catch an alert response before it is lost. Dangling a toy from a string can sometimes work

as well, especially if you attach the string to a yardstick, which gives you greater maneuverability.

Because cats like to curl up in small, enclosed spaces, you can place a basket or a box nearby and wait for the right pose. If your cat likes to sleep in the bathroom sink, your picture is made. Ditto the brown paper bag in which all cats love to play.

Catnip can be used to focus a cat's attention. The results are often hilarious, as the magical herb turns a cat on.

Using a table, indoors or out, often solves several problems at once: it keeps the animal in a lighted area, lets you shoot the picture at its eye level, and controls the background.

No subject is going to look its best if it is posed against a clump of shrubbery with leaves or twigs growing out of its head, or against flowered wallpaper. Keep backgrounds as simple and plain as possible.

If the animal is dark, try positioning it against a plain light wall, or if it's outdoors, against the sky. If it is a light-colored cat, place it against a plain dark background.

When photographing cats on the ground or floor, get down to their level, even if it means lying on your stomach. It is the animal's eyes that are the most expressive part of its face.

Soft light rather than bright sunlight, with its harsh contrasts of light and shadow, usually works better too. The exception to this rule is the all-black cat, which needs all the light it can get to avoid looking like a lump.

If you want a back-lighted profile of your cat, position it in a window and shoot from behind. This won't work if the sun is hitting your lens straight on, but at the right time of day, you can often catch an appealing pose.

A portrait of your cat means you must get in as close to the animal as you can. Most amateurs err in their shots of people or pets by standing twenty yards away instead of four or five feet, or even closer if your camera permits.

Instamatics allow four-foot close-ups, and shoot at 1/125th of a second. Remember, you are aiming at a living, high-strung animal, not the Grand Canyon.

*

If you are lucky enough to have a helper around, by all means make use of him or her as handler. Two heads and four hands are a great advantage over one and two. The helper concentrates on distracting the cat's attention; you concentrate on the photograph.

*

Never prolong the photography session past the animal's level of tolerance, no matter how short that may be. Fatigue will rapidly change to irritability, and who needs to memorialize a spit?

*

When the right moment comes, take several shots in rapid succession. The second or third one may be the winner.

Choosing a Veterinarian

Don't wait until your cat is sick before you choose a veterinarian. If Tabby has a bellyache in the middle of the night, after-hours emergency care is not generally available to strangers, only to established clients.

*

Before your cat's first checkup, find a veterinarian in your area. Ask responsible pet-caring friends and neighbors for the names of their veterinarians or call your local humane society or city animal-regulation department. Some veterinarians are better with cats than are others. Some even have exclusive feline practices.

*

After you, your cat's best friend will be its veterinarian. The time for that first meeting should be immediately after it comes to your house to stay, for a checkup and the beginning of its inoculations.

*

Be sure to make an appointment. Don't just go in off the street. A good veterinarian has as big a patient load as your family physician.

*

Tabby should always go to the animal hospital in her carrier. She's trembling enough already, and doesn't need a German shepherd lunging at her in the waiting room.

*

As soon as you and Tabby show up for her first appointment, you will have a pretty good idea if this veterinarian is worth waiting for. If the place obviously needs to be scrubbed down and if you need a gas mask just to sit in the waiting room, leave fast, kitty and caboodle. (It won't smell like a candy store, either, but it shouldn't stink.)

Is the receptionist friendly, intelligent, and courteous? Usually a good doctor is known by the employees he or she hires.

Once inside the treatment room, make sure the technician or assistant has either finished, or is in the process of, swabbing the examining table after the last patient. Basic hygiene is very important.

If the veterinarian picks up Tabby gently, soothes her nervousness by speaking softly and calling her by name as the member of the family that she is, you'll know this doctor has the proper sensitivity for his or her profession.

If all you have come for is shots, the doctor will explain to you what is being done, what disease Tabby will be protected against, and what boosters are needed and when. Write all this information down and make another appointment as you leave.

Even if all you have come for is inoculations, a first visit should also include a checkup of heart, ears, teeth, and a look-over for external parasites. The general health of the cat will be noticed in terms of coat condition, color of gums and ears, and demeanor.

If your cat is really ill, a better-than-average veterinarian always discusses the diagnosis in detail with you, asks for further tests, and may even let you watch the laboratory procedures.

A good veterinarian is also frank in admitting when he or she doesn't know the answer to your cat's problems, and will then suggest a consultation with another doctor.

Be sure to ask the veterinarian about fees. Don't wait until the bill comes and Tabby is glowing with good health again.

Cutting Down on the Cat Population

No one has ever taken a cat census, but estimates place the total at around forty million, give or take a few. Of these, at least ten million to fifteen million are homeless, living in alleys or in rural backwoods, existing on whatever scraps of food they can scrounge.

*

All pet cats—in the opinion of humane societies, veterinary groups, and other authorities on cats—should be neutered or spayed unless they are purebreds involved in professional breeding programs. To the best of my knowledge, other forms of birth control, such as steroids in the food, have not been tried with cats.

*

Science and Public Affairs (Bulletin of Atomic Scientists) reports that "about $125 million are spent annually to care for and dispose of unwanted animals" and that "approximately 13.3 million dogs and cats are destroyed each year at private and public shelters."

*

The Animal Protection Institute of America estimates that over $500 million is spent yearly for animal control. Many more die of starvation or disease or are killed by automobiles or other animals.

*

There are millions more pets than there are homes to take care of them, and the number is rising.

*

For every 415 people born every hour, says *Science and Public Affairs*, 2,000 to 3,500 dogs and cats are born.

*

At the present rate, one can estimate that there will be between 175 and 300 million cats and dogs in this country by the middle 1980s.

*

The whole scene is fast becoming what is called pet pollution.

*

While the problem is more easily controlled in dogs (they do not come in heat as often as cats, there are leash laws in most communities, and uncastrated male dogs can be deprived of a mate without any psychological or physical effects), the case for altering cats of both sexes is without serious argument.

175

*

Let's consider the female cat. In a year your queen will have at least two litters (sometimes as many as four), with an average of four kittens each. The second year, these cats will produce at least sixty-four kittens. Get out your calculator and figure out how many kittens will be born in ten years. The sum is staggering: over eighty million (assuming two litters per year, 2.8 surviving kittens per litter [evenly divided in gender], and ten years of breeding life)!

*

Even if you never allow your pet puss to roam, you are letting yourself in for a lot of static when she comes in season. Her yowling and pacing will drive all within hearing up the proverbial wall. Next, all the male cats for miles around will get the word and line up in your yard in hopes that their beloved will manage to slip out the door. They will add their voices to hers—and always after midnight.

*

If she is not allowed to breed, she is likely to come in heat again in a very short while and to keep on cycling until she finds a mate.

*

If unbred, your pet cat may develop endrometritis or pyometra—an accumulation of pus in the uterine cavity caused by closure of the cervix associated with a preceding inflammation.

*

Some veterinarians also report that other illnesses, such as diarrhea and convulsions, can sometimes be seen in the unspayed cat that is not allowed to mate.

*

Most owners of female cats are convinced that the only wise and humane course is to spay their pets.

*

Spaying is an operation best performed between six and eight months of age, though it can be done at any age and even if she has given birth before.

*

Technically it is called an ovariohysterectomy, in which both ovaries, both uterine horns, and most or all of the uterine body are removed. The cat is sedated prior to being spayed and completely anesthetized during the surgery.

*

She suffers little or no pain afterwards and is released to go home in twelve to forty-eight hours. (Some cats come home the evening of surgery—they may be a little groggy from the anesthetic, but are otherwise fine and able to eat a hearty breakfast the next morning.)

*

The argument that a spayed female will get fat and lazy after spaying is nonsense. She will only if you overfeed her. Most spayed cats are as sleek and beautiful as before surgery. And just as lively too.

*

The real controversy among cat owners arises over whether or not it is necessary to alter a *male* cat. And the protests are usually from men. (Oddly enough, women seldom object to spaying female cats.) Perhaps the men who oppose neutering their male cats are confusing their own sexuality with that of their pets. Neutering is necessary because an unaltered male cat is simply not a suitable pet. He will roam in search of a mate, become entangled in fights with other males over a female, and come home with torn jowls, mangled ears, or worse, or he will not come home at all.

*

The bad news continues: the urine of an unaltered male cat stinks to high heaven, and the odor will permeate any home, no matter how often one changes the litter pan.

*

An unaltered male cat will also spray. Spraying is a male cat's way of marking his territory or of expressing anxiety or displeasure (as when a new cat or baby is introduced into the family), and he will indulge in this habit either inside or outside the house.

*

A male cat will back up to a surface (your new chair, your shoe, a wall, the hedge) and urinate in a horizontal stream. It is his natural way of asserting dominance. (If you've ever had your front porch thoroughly sprayed by a neighbor's tomcat, you know how objectionable it is. Even skunk spray is preferable.)

*

The operation for altering or neutering a male cat is a simple one, consisting of the removal of both testicles. Your cat can come home the same day, and gives no evidence of discomfort.

*

The best age for castration is between seven and nine months, depending on the cat's rate of maturity. A cat needs his male hormones for skeletal development, but you don't want to wait until he has begun his tomcat habits.

Take Felix to your veterinarian at seven months or a little before. If your doctor decides he is ready for neutering, fine. If your cat is too immature, the doctor will tell you when to bring him back.

*

Even if you have acquired an adult cat, it is not too late to have him altered.

*

In a recent study by veterinarians at the School of Veterinary Medicine at the University of California at Davis, it was demonstrated that a pronounced and rapid postoperative decline in fighting, roaming, and urine spraying occurred in significant numbers of cases. Age at the time of castration was not related to the rate of decline.

*

A neutered male cat loses his aggressive fighting habits, but can still defend his rights if provoked.

*

He is gentler, but no sissy. He will not get fat or lose interest in life. He will just lose interest in sex. This cat will live longer, be healthier, bloom with catness. He will not impregnate hundreds upon hundreds of lady cats.

Ailurophobia

This is a fancy name for a morbid, irrational fear of cats. It is not an uncommon fear, as psychotherapists will testify. But the number of people who suffer from the phobia and never seek help far exceeds the number who are willing to be treated. To an ailurophobe, all cats, even the most gentle, are man-eating tigers. Or, as sometimes happens with spiders and snakes, objects of enormous, unexplained revulsion.

*

An ailurophobe cannot sit in the same room with a cat, will cross the street to avoid a cat sauntering down the avenue, and in extreme cases, cannot even hold a picture of a cat without dropping it and showing symptoms of trembling, rapid heartbeat, and sweating.

*

Many ailurophobes use the same phrase in describing their dread of a cat: "I can't stand her eyes. She looks right through me!"

*

White cats are less intimidating to an ailurophobe than black ones.

*

The cause behind ailurophobia can be one of several: a hangover from either the negative myths cats have always been associated with—witches, bad luck, demons, Satan—or tales told a child by a mother who was similarly conditioned. It can also be the direct result of a bad encounter with a cat that clawed the person when he was a child or pounced on him unexpectedly. We are always afraid of what surprises us, and cats are notoriously quick to move.

*

Some authorities, such as Theodore Reik, the psychoanalyst, believe fear of cats is associated with sexual fears. To this idea the behaviorist school of psychology gives a loud snort, saying that the Freudians frequently want to reduce everything to sex.

*

The behaviorists do not believe that searching for the remote cause, be it real or symbolic, and then talking about it, is going to relieve anyone of the phobia. Their treatment is the same for all patients afflicted with this irrational fear, regardless of the cause: a program of desensitization.

*

The patient learns first how to relax through breathing techniques, and how to slow the heartbeat through biofeedback instruments.

*

The next step is to build a hierarchy of scenes in the imagination, beginning with the least threatening picture the patient can conceive—a dead cat a block away, for instance—and moving step by step to the most threatening—a cat in the patient's arms. At every step the patient's reactions are monitored by a polygraph instrument, and at the first sign of anxiety the image is removed by suggestion and relaxation reintroduced.

*

Imagination therapy is followed by watching movies of cats—again, starting with a sleeping kitten and gradually advancing in hierarchal order to close-ups of an adult cat running toward the camera. The film will be run many times, always accompanied by careful monitoring of the patient's emotional responses. When there is a nice, flat line on the polygraph, the patient is ready for therapy *in vivo*.

*

A live cat is put in a room next to the doctor's office. The patient can observe the cat clearly but is protected by a glass wall from any physical contact. Anxiety is monitored as before.

*

The cat is then brought into the doctor's office and controlled by an attendant at some distance from the patient. Gradually the patient progresses from merely observing the cat across the room being petted by the attendant, to putting his gloved hand on top of the therapist's as he pets the cat, to putting a bare hand on the doctor's hand, to putting his own bare hand on the cat.

*

Total time for the cure: about twenty-eight weeks, give or take a week, depending on the patient.

Pros and Cons of Euthanasia

On the subject of euthanasia every pet-owner has strong feelings. It is a topic of such enormous sensitivity, bordering as it does on that of love and loss, that very few people agree on anything. There are certain points of view that can be discussed. We need all the enlightenment we can get.

Appropriate

Although every case should be considered individually, I am of the opinion—as are most veterinarians I know—that euthanasia is only appropriate when the animal is suffering a terminal and painful illness such as cancer, or some other hopeless condition that cannot possibly be treated medically or surgically. Kidney failure, so often present in cases of old age, brings it under this category. Uremic poisoning is not a happy way to go.

*

I am also in favor of euthanasia when the animal is so old and feeble that it can no longer enjoy its simple pleasures of eating and interacting with its human family.

Inappropriate

There are other veterinarians—and pet owners—who believe in euthanasia for pets that are, for one reason or another, considered incorrigible or antisocial.

*

Even cats who only scratch the furniture or soil the rug are sometimes "put to sleep" (a euphemism I do not care for) rather than retrained.

*

Other reasons of expediency rather than the animal's welfare are used as excuses for euthanasia by some owners: the family is moving and no longer wants a pet; the owner has died and the heirs can't be bothered with Felix;

Mama Cat has had babies and it is too much trouble to find homes for them.

*

An elderly lady I know has a young, healthy, easily-adoptable cat, yet in her will has instructed her executor to have the animal euthanized. In the mistaken belief that the cat would not survive without her, she stubbornly refuses to revise her instructions. This, in my opinion, is a distorted sense of compassion, but it is not uncommon.

*

As for too many progeny, it used to be customary to drown or chloroform all such, and this practice is still common in rural communities. Today we preach neutering and spaying as preventive measures, and if those fail, recommend that sincere efforts be made to find proper homes for the kittens, and that the parent animals be altered before another pregnancy takes place.

*

To find a proper home for that kitten takes a little effort, a lot of patience, and a dash of pizzaz.

*

Many veterinarians also take the trouble to find homes for unwanted animals, often without fanfare or publicity, for fear their offices will be used as dumping grounds.

*

I know one animal hospital that often has a cute kitten sleeping in the Out basket on the reception desk. It doesn't take long before someone finds it irresistible, and another life is saved.

*

The alternative *worse* than euthanasia is to dump the small animals along the road, in strange neighborhoods, hoping someone else will be more charitable than the dumper. A pox on him. The large majority of such animals are either killed by cars, die of starvation and exposure, or become feral. Only a tiny fraction ever find loving homes.

On the Other Hand . . .

Some owners delay euthanasia when it would be the humane decision to make, or forego it entirely in the mistaken idea that all animals should die a "natural" death.

*

That their cat is obviously in incurable misery concerns some owners less than their own revulsion at death.

Death is life's one inevitability. Why not make it as easy and merciful for our pets as we can?

Who Makes the Decision?

Reputable veterinarians seem to agree that this most sensitive of all decisions must be made by the owner, not by the doctor.

*

True, the vet can point out all the pros and cons and thus help you make up your mind, but it is you who must face up to the decision, whatever it is, and live with it.

*

Above all, you should not be hurried in your conclusion. The matter is too heavy a one; the pain too great.

*

When I took my old cat, Cinnamon, to the hospital for what I thought would be treatment of a minor lameness, I had suddenly to face the awful fact that he had osteosarcoma and that it had spread to the lungs. The kind doctor showed me the X-rays.

*

I had had Cinnamon and his mother for a span of twenty years. Daffodil had finally gone, but I could not imagine life without old Cinnamon. The doctor gently assured me Cinnamon's case was hopeless, that it would be downhill all the way. And still he didn't hurry me.

*

That wrenching goodbye was one of the hardest I ever had to say; a hypodermic syringe of pentobarbital sodium performed its work quickly and painlessly. Though I was crying so hard I could hardly find the door, I knew I had done what was right for Cinnamon.

*

I know some owners who have always euthanized their own animals, preferring to administer the last rites themselves, at home, where the pet is less likely to be frightened. I salute such people; I haven't the guts for it myself.

*

To all pet owners or potential owners, I urge you to treat euthanasia as a privilege for your animals, not to be taken lightly but not to be ignored.

If it has to be used, don't then be reluctant to adopt another animal that needs a home. Turn your grief into love for another creature that needs it— just as badly as the one you lost.

About the Author

As contributing editor of *Woman's Day* since 1973, Jean Burden has written a regular column on pets of all kinds—from cats and dogs to gerbils and parakeets—but her first love has always been cats. She has five other books in the pet field, all in print, with sales exceeding two million copies. She is also well-known as a poet. Her first collection of poems *Naked as the Glass* was published in 1963, and her book of essays on the creative process *Journey toward Poetry* came out three years later. Sometimes the two aspects of her life come together as when in 1974 she edited an anthology of poems titled *A Celebration of Cats*. She has over a thousand articles to her credit, ranging widely over the fields of animal welfare, poetry, modern architecture and oriental religion. She has been active in the American Humane Association, Morris Animal Foundation, and currently serves on the board of directors of Pet Pride. She lives in Southern California in a red and white farmhouse with two cats—naturally.

Index

186

conjunctivitis, 34, 50
constipation, 38
courage, in cats, 109
curiosity, in cats, 111–12
curtains, in cages, 28
curaneous larva migrans, 81
cystitis, 129

daffodils, 154
deafness, 166
death, euthanasia and, 180–83
de-clawing, 121
dehydration, 72
demodectic mange (red mange), 53
deworming, 81
diabetes, 47, 166
Diana (deity), 12
diarrhea, 38–39
dieffenbachias, 154
diet, see feeding; food
discipline for cats, 117–18
diseases, see illnesses
distemper (panleukopenia), 41–44
    not transmitted to humans, 81
dogs, 14
    affection in, 107
    cats chased by, 109
    cats compared with, 137–40
    diets of, 88
    distemper in, 42
    fleas and, 66–68
    population of, 175
    relationships between cats and, 115,
        132–34, 149
domestication of cats, history of, 11
drugs
    administration of, 71–72
    aspirin, 75–76
    for fleas, 68–69

ear mites, 31–32, 53, 63
ears, 31–33
    frostbite of, 60
    grooming and, 62–63
    movements of, 141–42
    odotectic mange of, 53
    solar dermatitis of, 54

eggs, 85
Egypt, cats in, 11–12
Egyptian Mau, 17
elderly cats, 73–77
elephant's ears (plant), 154
emetics, 157
endrometritis, 176
England (Britain)
    history of cat breeding in, 13
    history of cats in, 11
    quarantines of pets in, 162
eosinophilic granuloma, 54
epilepsy, 47, 166
ESP (extrasensory perception), in cats,
    109–10, 144–46
estrus (in heat), 93
    catnip and, 124
Europe, history of cats in, 11
euthanasia, 180–83
exercise, for elderly cats, 76–77
exotic shorthair, 17
extrasensory perception (ESP), in cats,
    109–10, 144–46
eyelids, 33
eyes
    communications through, 142
    health of, 33–34
    of pedigreed cats, 14
eye stains, 63

falls, 48, 106
false pregnancy, 103
fat cats, 76, 88–89, 106
fear of cats, 178–80
feeding, 83–91
    of orphan kittens, 99–100
    overeating and, 106
    overfeeding and, 156
    pica and, 130–31
    in prenatal care, 94–95
    while traveling, 161, 162
    weaning of kittens and, 100–2
    see also food
feline acne, 53
feline caliciviral disease (FCD), 49
feline distemper (panleukopenia), 41–44
    not transmitted to humans, 81

housebreaking, 116, 127–9
    cleaning and, 129–30
Household Pet Class, 27
house plants, 154, 157
humans
    babies of, cats and, 105
    brain of, 109
    fears of cats in, 178–80
    fleas and, 66
    illnesses transmitted from cats to,
        78–82
    neutering of cats and, 177
    oriented towards cats or dogs, 137–40
hunting, by cats, 12–13, 113
hyacinths, 154

illnesses
    home care for, 70–73
    transmitted to humans from cats,
        78–82
    see also health
inoculations, 26, 41, 174
    against feline leukemia virus, 46
    against feline respiratory problems,
        49–51
    on interstate health certificates, 158,
        161
    against panleukopenia, 43–44
insecticides, 153
intelligence, in cats, 109–11
international travel, 162
interstate health certificates, 158
ivy, 154

Japan, history of cats in, 11, 18
Japanese bobtail, 17–18
jasmine, 154
jimson weeds, 154
judges, at cat shows, 29

Kaffir (Caffre) cats, 11
kennels, 165–66
kidney failure, 180
kitchens, keeping cats out of, 152–53
Kitten Class, 27
Kitten Milk Replacement (KMR),
    99–100

kittens, 93–104
    cataracts in, 34
    children and, 147–48
    falls by, 106
    feeding of, 84–87, 90
    grooming of, 61
    in hot weather, 58
    housebreaking of, 116, 128
    not available for Christmas, 157
    panleukopenia in, 42, 44
    pulse rates in, 71
    purring by, 35
    as second pets, 132–34
    shopping for, 22–26
    toxoplasmosis in, 79
    training against scratching in, 120
    worms in, 39
KMR (Kitten Milk Replacement),
    99–100
Korat, 18

labor, 96–98
larva migrans, 81
laurels, 154
laxatives, 38
learning, in cats, 110–11
leashes, 118
leukemia, 45–46
    not transmitted to humans from cats,
        81
lifting of cats and kittens, 101–2, 147
lily of the valley, 154
linear granuloma, 54
litter pans, 127–28
liver, 38
longhair cats
    breeds of, 20–22
    fleas on, 66
    grooming of, 61–62
longhaired Siamese (Balinese), 20
"longy" manx, 18
lost cats, 167–70
lungworms, 39
lymphosarcoma, 45

mackerel tabby, 15
Maine coon cat, 20–21

Spector, Ira, 146
spraying, 35, 129, 177, 178
    cleaning after, 130
steatitis, 85
stomachworms, 39
stud tail, 64, 65
Supilak, 21

tabby cats, 14–15
tails, 141
tapeworms, 39
    spread by fleas, 67, 70
tartar, 36, 63
tattooing, 170
taurine, 88
teeth, 36–37, 63
temperament, of kittens, 104
temperature, in cats, 71
tender loving care (TLC)
    for elderly cats, 77
    for ill cats, 73
Teutonic cults, 12
Thailand, cats in, 18
thiaminase, 88
threadworms, 39
toes, polydactylism of, 37
toilet bowls, water from, 84
Toxoplasma gondii, 79
toxoplasmosis, 79–80
toys, 113–14
training
    of cats, 116–19
    of dogs and cats compared, 138–39
trains, 163
traveling, 160–63
    interstate health certificates for, 158
trees, cats in, 122–23
tumors, 44
Turkish Angora, 21

United States, cat associations in, 13

urinary problems (feline urologic
    syndrome; FUS), 54–56, 129

vaccinations, *see* inoculations
vegetarian cats, 88
veterinarians
    at cat shows, 28, 29
    choosing, 173–74
    elderly cats and, 75, 76
    on euthanasia, 180–82
    initial checkups by, 26, 104
    moving and, 158–61
    panleukopenia and, 43
    prenatal care by, 95
Victoria (queen, England), 19
visceral larva migrans, 81
vision, of cats, 33, 106
    blindness and, 167
vitamins, 86
    for preventing fleas, 69–70
vocal cords, 35
vomiting, 40

water, 76, 84, 95, 101
    cats' attitudes toward, 112
    traveling and, 162
Way, T., 74
weaning, 100–2
weather
    hot, 58–59
    winter, 59–60
Weigel, I., 33
whipworms, 39
whiskers, 62
winter dangers, 59–60
witchcraft, cats associated with, 12
worms, 39–40
    spread by fleas, 67, 70
    transmitted to humans from cats, 81

zoonosis, 78